Fall

Growing in Christ™

Parents & Twos

A Christ-Centered Curriculum for Parents and Their Toddlers

TEACHER GUIDE

CONCORDIA PUBLISHING HOUSE • SAINT LOUIS

3558 S. Jefferson Ave., St. Louis, MO 63118-3968
1-800-325-3040 • www.cph.org

Written by Jane Haas

Edited by Pamela Nielsen

This publication may be available in braille, in large print, or on cassette tape for the visually impaired. Please allow 8 to 12 weeks for delivery. Write to the Library for the Blind, 7550 Watson Rd., St. Louis, MO 63119-4409; call toll-free 1-888-215-2455; or visit the Web site: www.blindmission.org.

Growing in Christ™ is published quarterly by Concordia Publishing House. Your comments and suggestions concerning this material are appreciated. E-mail us at sundayschool@cph.org.

Manufactured in the United States of America

Contents

*Craft Pages, Family Pages, and other resources can be found on the Teacher CD.

Welcome to Growing in Christ!

Jesus says,

> **"Already you are clean because of the word that I have spoken to you. Abide in Me, and I in you. As the branch cannot bear fruit by itself, unless it abides in the vine, neither can you, unless you abide in Me. I am the vine; you are the branches." John 15:3–5**

GROWING IN CHRIST is the life of the child of God! Through the Word and Sacraments, we live and grow in Christ.

GROWING IN CHRIST is a Sunday School curriculum rich in God's holy Word. Students learn all the major stories of the Old and New Testaments and see how God weaves His plan of salvation in Christ through the lives of ordinary men, women, and children.

GROWING IN CHRIST puts the focus squarely on the heart and center of the entire Bible: Jesus Christ, our Savior from sin, death, and the devil. Each lesson reveals our sin and God's forgiving mercy in Christ.

GROWING IN CHRIST lessons connect the Word of God to the daily life of the student, nurturing faith in our loving, forgiving Savior.

GROWING IN CHRIST strengthens Christ-centered grateful response in lives marked by thanks and praise and service and obedience.

GROWING IN CHRIST teaches the language and shape of Christian faith and life in the Lutheran Church, grounding students in the Bible, Small Catechism, and hymnal.

GROWING IN CHRIST is filled with age-appropriate activities and teaching tools that engage children in meaningful, relevant interaction with God's Word.

GROWING IN CHRIST provides flexible teaching options, adaptable for local circumstances, giving teachers the choice to use what works best for them. In your classroom, you are the expert. You know the children and their abilities, so you choose what works best.

GROWING IN CHRIST is the life of the child of God!

Introduction

Why Have a Parents & Twos Sunday School Class?

God gives primary responsibility to parents to instruct their children in all His ways. Moses instructed parents in the way they should teach their children about God when he wrote God's inspired words in Deuteronomy 6:4–9:

> *The* Lord *our God, the* Lord *is one. You shall love the* Lord *your God with all your heart and with all your soul and with all your might. And these words that I command you today shall be on your heart. You shall teach them diligently to your children, and shall talk of them when you sit in your house, and when you walk by the way, and when you lie down, and when you rise. You shall bind them as a sign on your hand, and they shall be as frontlets between your eyes. You shall write them on the doorposts of your house and on your gates.*

These Scripture verses emphasize the importance of God's directive to parents to bring their children up in the nurture of His Word and in fellowship with Christians:

> *Train up a child in the way he should go; and when he is old he will not depart from it (Proverbs 22:6).*
>
> *[Joseph and Mary took Jesus] to Jerusalem to present Him to the Lord (Luke 2:22).*
>
> *The child [Jesus] grew and became strong, filled with wisdom. And the favor of God was upon Him (Luke 2:40).*
>
> *[Jesus said,] "Let the children come to Me, and do not hinder them, for to such belongs the kingdom of God (Luke 18:16).*

Each waking moment parents are to grab the opportunity to talk about God, His love and forgiveness for us through His Son, Jesus, always keeping Him in front of their children so they can see how great God is and what great things He has done for us—especially His great gift of salvation through Jesus' death and resurrection.

Parents need help. Pastors, teachers, and lay people in the church can help train parents to train their children. *Parents & Twos* can both help welcome and meet the needs of families with toddlers.

Many families live far from relatives, may feel isolated, and need the encouragement and support of Christian friends in the church community.

God's Church becomes a special, familiar place for toddlers when they attend worship services and Parents & Twos class with their parents. The faith that began in them through Baptism is nurtured and strengthened when very young children hear God's Word, participate in activities related to the Bible story, sing, pray, and praise God.

What Is Parents & Twos?

- A Christ-centered education program for parents and their two-year-olds
- An opportunity to meet as a small group to learn together of God's love for all people through the life, death, and resurrection of His Son, Jesus
- Age-appropriate learning experiences for toddlers
- A relationship-building time for families who have very young children

- A time for parents to see their faith through the eyes of their children; a time to help them see more clearly their role as Christian parents

Getting to Know Two-Year-Olds

Twos:

- Are egocentric, thinking the world revolves around them
- Have a difficult time sharing
- Play parallel to each other
- Need routine and need to know what to expect
- Use their whole bodies to learn about the world around them
- Need space, equipment, and action experiences to meet their large motor needs
- Need a variety of hands-on learning and discovering activities
- Need solid, concrete items to help them learn
- Aren't able to sit still for very long
- Need not be potty trained to participate in this class
- Enjoy the process of doing projects more than the actual finished project
- Can use chunky crayons and markers to scribble-color
- Do not have the fine motor skills to use scissors yet
- Need much repetition in learning
- Enjoy moving to music
- May or may not communicate with words yet
- Learn through sensory experiences
- Learn best through play—children's work
- Experience God's love through adults who demonstrate it

The Parent-Child Relationship

During the Activity Center time, parents and their children experiment, discover, and learn by using the materials in each center.

- Print the day's lesson focus on a chalkboard, white board, or poster for the parents to see.
- Speak to parents through their children. "Tara, can you show Daddy the new puzzles?"
- Model appropriate adult responses to the children's activities. When Jude puts a pan of play dough into the oven, the teacher says, "Mmmm, something smells good over here. Who is baking something delicious?"
- Emphasize that it's a time to do something with their children, not for them.
- Create signs (if needed) to help parents focus on each activity and its purpose (i.e., Help your child color the art page; Talk about how good God is to make the world and our bodies; Place stickers on the page too; Thank You, God, for making Your world and for making me!).
- During Parent Talk time children may have their snacks. Those who are comfortable leaving the table after eating and playing in a separate corner of the room with another adult or teen supervising, may do so. Children who don't want to be separated from parents may stay at the snack table and make the transition to a play dough or puzzle activity after eating.
- Parents can enjoy their two-year-olds more if they learn to understand them. Use the Parent Talk time to be supportive and encouraging, to share Scripture and what

God says to Christian parents, and to provide ideas for Christian parents in their daily child raising.

Creating a Child-Appropriate Environment

- Be sure the area/room is safe. Check for electrical outlets and any sharp corners or other hazards.
- Open space is most needed for active learning. An area rug for storytelling time works well.
- Have child-size tables and chairs as well as chairs for parents to sit comfortably.
- Open wall space is needed for poster and picture hanging. Be sure to use putty or adhesive that doesn't remove paint from the wall.
- Define areas for each Activity Center and keep them the same each week so children know what to expect.
- Create a worship/storytelling area in a quiet corner. Put a tablecloth or sheet over a short table or sturdy box. Place an unbreakable cross and vase of flowers on the "altar." Provide appropriate color strips to match the colors of your church's altar paraments. Hang the portrait of Jesus. Use an area rug, quilt, or blanket for seating. Place a CD player close by.

Teacher Tools and Family Kit

Features of this Teacher Guide

- Easy to use, four-step weekly lesson plans
- Learning activities, songs and hymns, transition activities, action rhymes, resources
- "Teacher talk" is in bold print to provide you with words as a model for the parents to use with their children.

Pick and choose learning activities, songs, and action rhymes that fit the needs of the children in your group. Much repetition is necessary when teaching very young children. Toddlers learn best by repetition!

Features of the Teacher CD

- **Songs and action rhymes:** Suggestions are provided in each lesson. Play the CD and sing along. As you repeat the songs, hymns, and portions of the liturgy, along with the action rhymes throughout the quarter, children will slowly begin to participate in singing and saying the words. Don't expect them to sing or talk if they are young Twos. Their language development takes time.
- **Craft Pages:** One coloring page is provided for each lesson. The teacher will need to supply crayons, glue sticks, and stickers for families to use. Consider doing the extra option suggestions in the art activities so that the children aren't always scribble-coloring on one-dimensional paper.
- **Family Info Page:** Have a parent (or adult) from each family complete this page at the beginning of the quarter so you have pertinent information about the child and family.
- **Family Pages:** Each has reinforcement activities and ideas for the families. Duplicate these and send home after each class.

Posters

- These colorful visuals are used throughout the quarter to teach and reinforce the lessons. They will last a long time if you laminate and carefully store them.

Features of the Family Kit

- **Child's Bible Storybook**—a review of the quarterly lessons with visuals and text
- **CD** of songs, Scripture, and action rhymes

Sprout the Puppet

Sprout is one of the puppets in the Growing in Christ Early Childhood materials. You may order Sprout from Concordia Publishing House (Order No. 41-1027). If you don't have Sprout, you may substitute any puppet you have.

Teacher Tip

Welcome families to bring their infants also. They sometimes sleep in a baby carrier in a safe corner, and when awake, they enjoy hearing the music and the activities.

Getting Started

- **Pray.** Ask that God will bless your efforts and be with you and your helpers as you minister to the families and their very young children.
- **Start Small.** Check your congregation's cradle roll and baptismal records for names of children. If you have a long list of children, begin with the older Twos. In person or on the phone, talk with each family that has a toddler and invite them to the class. Follow up with a mailed invitation. As your class becomes established, expect walk-ins and give them a warm welcome!
- **Publicize.** Place an informational paragraph about the class and its purpose in your church's bulletin, newsletter, and on a bulletin board about children's ministry. Hang an eye-appealing sign outside your classroom, post photos of families participating in activities together, and invite grandparents and congregational members to an open house. Ask parents to tell about the blessings they experience through the class to other small groups, to a congregational meeting, or before a worship service.
- **Pastor.** Ask your pastor(s) to include prayers for the Parents & Twos class during the worship services.
- **Two Teachers.** This is the best scenario for a Parents & Twos class. Two teachers can help provide "teacher talk" for parents and children during the Activity Center time, and also during snack and Parent Talk time.
- **Secure Environment.** Two-year-olds bloom within a secure environment (including the same smiling faces to welcome them each class session).
- **Involve Parents.** Often parents are more than willing to help with setup/put-away and also bring snacks.
- **Family Information.** Gather family information by having a parent complete a Family Info Page (Teacher CD). The information will help you remember to celebrate special occasions and identify any allergies the child may have. Ask families for their permission to share their e-mail addresses and phone numbers with families in the group.
- **Nametags.** Make nametags for each parent and child. (Use these until names are familiar.)
- **Advance the Threes.** Prepare to advance newly turned three-year-olds to the next class as little groups, if possible, because of the friendships children form. You might do this monthly or quarterly or ask the Early Childhood level teachers for the best time to transition the children. Advancement should always depend on the readiness of each child.
- **Evaluate.** It is helpful to evaluate your class on an ongoing basis. Ask teachers, helpers, parents, and others involved to help evaluate the Parents & Twos ministry.

Teacher Tip

Teachers of young children are special people who focus on the children and their needs. These teachers need to be dedicated and reliable. They should have a heart for families who have very young children and believe in the importance of sharing the Gospel message.

- What are our major strengths?
- What are our major weaknesses?
- How well are we meeting the needs of the children? (Scale 1–6)
- How well are we meeting the parents' needs?
- Are we reaching all relevant families in our congregation?
- Are we reaching out to our community?
- What is one thing we can do to improve our educational program?

God Is with You!

- Regularly frequent God's house to receive His gifts in Word and Sacrament.
- Remember that God works through you by His Holy Spirit through His Word as you teach and model it for the children.
- Pray for God's direction, words to say, and the strength and courage to lead each class.
- Remember you are part of His plan to "go and make disciples of all nations, baptizing them in the name of the Father and of the Son and of the Holy Spirit, and teaching them to obey everything I have commanded you. And surely I am with you always, to the very end of the age" (Matthew 28:19–20). Trust God to help you!

The Importance of Balancing Law and Gospel

We all need forgiveness. Daily our sins separate us from God, our heavenly Father. We say we are sorry. And because of the suffering and death of His Son, Jesus, God forgives us. He brings us close to Him again. What a wonderful, loving, forgiving Father we have!

Young children live in a world filled with the Law. Each day they're confronted with their sins and their limitations. They live in a world filled with noes and don'ts. The Law is very real to them. Even though they are very young, two-year-olds can still experience the separation that sin causes between God and us. They can't understand that God can still love them despite the wrong things they do. They think they must do good in order to be loved. And when they fail to do good things, they feel unloved and alone. It's frightening for them! Two-year-olds daily need the reassurance of God's constant and forgiving love, just as their parents and ALL adults do. You can model this forgiving love.

To help Twos and their parents learn about Law and Gospel, you will want to model it with your own actions in the classroom. The boundaries you set up will provide the children with a safe environment of exploring and learning. As you teach (discipline) the children with love and forgiveness, you show them God's unconditional love. This helps make His love concrete for the children.

When children do something wrong, be sure to explain that you don't like the bad thing they've done, but you still love and forgive them as Jesus does. (Be careful not to say that they are "bad children"!) Say, "I don't like what you did. It was wrong to take the toy away from Sarah. But I love you, and I forgive you. Jesus loves and forgives you too." A hug helps to demonstrate this unconditional love along with your words. Children will then feel close to you and to Jesus once again.

When teaching children about good things they can do, be certain you don't give them the idea that in order for God to be happy they must do good deeds. Rather, they can show how much Jesus loves them by the good things they do. (Be sure to check any Christian storybooks you want to read to the children to avoid this kind of moralism.)

Tell the Gospel—the Good News—every time you are in class together. God's forgiving love is the central message you want the children and their parents to hear.

They need to know that He will always love and forgive them. They are His beloved children!

A Suggested Class Schedule

Opening—Relationship Building and Activity Centers (25 minutes)

- Give families the opportunity to get to know each other and participate with their children in the day's Activity Centers, which focus on the lesson's Gospel-centered theme.

Singing Circle (5 minutes)

- Celebrate children's birthdays and baptismal birthday anniversaries.
- Sing praise songs and have children move to music as they use rhythm instruments, ribbons, or scarves.

God Speaks—Introduce, Tell, and Apply the Bible Story—Snack Time (10 minutes)

- Children sit on a parent's lap or on a special rug or blanket.
- Sprout helps to introduce the Bible story.
- The leader uses an open Bible to tell a very brief Bible story and shows visuals.
- Apply the Bible story to the families' lives. Use simple words. Make a simple concrete connection with what the children already know and have heard.
- Pray together. Keep prayer phrases very short.
- Link to the liturgy by playing the CD as everyone moves to the table for snacks or at other transitional times.
- Provide simple, nutritious snacks. (Parents are often more than happy to help provide snacks. You might have a sign-up paper, listing lesson titles and giving snack suggestions that relate to the day's theme.)

We Live—Growing through God's Word—Parent Talk (10 minutes)

- Share Scripture and discuss Christian parenting ideas and resources.
- If you have a team teacher, share the responsibilities of leading the parents' group discussion and the children's playtime in a separate corner.

Closing (10 minutes)

- Review the day's Gospel-centered focus.
- Say an action rhyme and a short prayer.
- Sing a good-bye song.
- It's important to say a personal good-bye and give a hug as each child leaves with his or her parents. Say a simple focus statement such as "God made you and He cares for you, Rick." (Sprout can help you say good-byes to the children.)
- Invite families to return for the next class.
- Send home the child's Craft Page and the Family Page.

Lesson 1

God Made the World— God Made Me

Genesis 2

Key Point

God is so good. God made the whole world and God made me!

Connections

Bible Words
[God] cares for you. 1 Peter 5:7

Faith Words
God, Jesus, maker

Catechism
Apostles' Creed: First Article
I believe in God the Father Almighty, Maker of heaven and earth.

Liturgy
Thank the Lord and sing His praise; tell everyone what He has done.

Hymn
All Creatures of Our God and King (*Lutheran Worship* 436)

Materials Needed

Step		Materials
1 Opening	Teacher Tools	Nametags Family Info Page CD Craft Page 1: God Made My Body
	Other Supplies	See "To Prepare" instructions for each Activity Center Rhythm ribbons or scarves
2 God Speaks	Teacher Tools	Sprout puppet Teacher CD God Made Adam and Eve Poster Craft Page 1: God Made My Body
	Other Supplies	Toddler Bible Poster of Jesus Cross sticker for Sprout Inflated balloon Large mirror
3 We Live	Teacher Tools	Bible
4 Closing	Teacher Tools	Family Page 1
	Other Supplies	Toddler Bible

1 Opening
30 minutes

Welcome

Welcome families warmly by saying their names, getting down to the children's eye level. Tell them your name. Have parents create a nametag for each family member.

Introduce families to each other. Allow friendship-building time (important for growing relationships) at the beginning and end of each class.

Ask each family to complete a Family Info Page (found on the Teacher CD) for you to keep in your file. Especially note children's birth dates and baptismal dates as well as any allergies children may have.

Point out the main theme for today and explain that parents will want to reinforce the Bible truth with their children during the Activity Center time.

Encourage parents to spend time with their children at the Activity Centers, focusing on thanking God for making our wonderful bodies and His whole world.

Teacher Tip
To keep your quarterly materials organized, you might want to buy a large storage container with a sturdy lid for each quarter and label each, such as "Parents & Twos Fall Quarter; Parents & Twos Winter Quarter" and so on.

Activity Centers

Water

To Prepare: Vinyl tablecloth, plastic pan, measuring cups, funnels, scoops

Cover a table with the tablecloth and place a plastic pan with about 3 inches of water on the tablecloth. Provide measuring cups, small funnels, and plastic scoops. Have a towel or paper towels at this area.

Say **Water is fun and relaxing. Swish your hands in the water. Look what you can do with your hands! You can pour water from one cup to another. You can scoop water into a cup. God made the water and God made your hands. God made everything!**

Art

To Prepare: Craft Page 1: God Made My Body; fabric swatches; cross stickers.

Duplicate the "God Made My Body" page. Have parents help their children color the page. Ask parents to print their children's names in a corner of the paper.

Say **Look at the shape on your paper. Point to the head. Point to the arms—one, two. Where are the legs? Can you find the feet? The hands? God made your body. He gave you a head, legs, arms, hands, and feet too. Thank You, God!**

Add a cross sticker to your paper. God loves us so much! So much that He sent Jesus to be our Savior and Friend. The cross reminds us of that.

Provide a few fabric swatches to glue onto the body for clothing. Use a glue stick rather than liquid glue since a child can hold and control the glue stick better.

Teacher Tip
Chunky crayons are best for very small hands to hold. As the kids color, remind parents not to expect toddlers to color inside lines or to add realistic facial features or clothing. At this age, scribble-coloring is what they do best!

Play Dough

To Prepare: Play dough; rolling pins; cookie cutters; plastic knives; craft sticks for cutting.

Set out various colors of play dough, child-size rolling pins, and cookie cutters of people, animals, flowers, a circle, and a cross.

Say **Squeeze and roll the play dough with your hands and arms. God gave you hands and arms to roll the play dough!**

Cut a play dough body shape. God made your body.

Use the circle to cut a play dough head. God made your head and face. Where is your head?

Roll play dough into leg shapes. God gave you legs and feet to walk and run!

Roll and cut other shapes. The cross reminds us that Jesus loves us so much that He died and came alive for us!

Discovery

To Prepare: Precut pictures of babies, children, adults, baby Jesus.

Glue precut magazine pictures of babies, children, and adults in a variety of activities such as sitting, standing, or jumping onto a large background paper.

Ask **What is this baby doing? God made her body. She can crawl. She can sit.**

What is this boy doing? Look at him running! He can chase a ball. God made your body and legs to run and chase.

What is this mommy doing? She can bat the ball! God made her arms and body to swing and hit a ball.

Who is this special baby? It's Jesus, who came to be our Savior!

Pretend

To Prepare: Baby dolls; kitchen play items; blocks; trucks and cars.

As children take care of the baby dolls,

Say **We're so glad God made our bodies. Where are your doll's toes? Where are your toes? God made your toes.** Continue with other body parts. **You're taking good care of your baby doll. God made us and He takes good care of us.**

As children play, comment about the parts of their bodies they are using.

Say **Look how high you have built the block wall! God made your arms to reach so high.**

Books and Puzzles

Simple shape and color puzzles; peg puzzles of people of all ages

Picture and board books about God's creation

Teacher Tip

Even very young children (not to mention their parents) appreciate knowing what to expect. They will adapt quickly to your class routine. Consider giving two-minute warnings.

Transition

1, 2

Tell families when two minutes or so remain so they can finish what they are doing.

When it's time to wrap-up, give children and parents two or three minutes to help put Activity Center items away as everyone sings "Let's Clean Up" (CD, tracks 1, 2) and moves to the Singing Circle area.

Singing Circle

Singing Circle time is a wonderful opportunity to sing together, move to music, have children wave colorful scarves or ribbons with songs of praise, and do simple actions to the lyrics. You'll find songs on the Teacher CD and on the Family CD. Choose a few songs to fit the needs of your families. Repeat the songs often.

Teacher Tip
Provide a special rug, blanket, or quilt in front of your altar as a sitting area for the children.

Teacher Tip
Speaking the invocation and making the sign of the cross each week will help the children to learn these important words.

Teacher Tip
Use your normal voice when speaking as the puppet. The children's imagination will help them think the puppet is talking. Have Sprout whisper into your ear sometimes to help the children focus on what the puppet wants to say.

Sing **First Article Song**
Morning Prayer Song
All Creatures of Our God and King
1 Peter 5:7
Good Morning to You
Happy Birthday and **God Made Me His Child** to celebrate birthdays and baptismal anniversaries.
I Can Stamp
Jesus Loves the Little Ones
He's Got the Whole World in His Hands (Variation: "He's Got the Girls and the Boys in His Hands")
God Is So Good (Variation: "God Makes Me His . . . He's So Good to Me.")

2 God Speaks
10 minutes

Come to the Worship Center

Have children sit in front of your altar to get ready to hear today's Bible story. Sing or hum "God Is So Good" as everyone gathers. Thank everyone for coming so nicely and for being ready to listen.

Say **Boys and girls, I am so glad you are here today to learn about our loving God. When we come together to learn about God, we begin in this very special way:**

In the name of the Father and of the Son and of the Holy Spirit. Amen.

Say these special words with me.

Repeat the invocation and make the sign of the cross by putting your fingers to your forehead, then your chest then one shoulder and then to the other shoulder.

Introducing God's Word

Introduce Sprout as you begin to interact with the puppet and the children. Sprout should wear a cross necklace or a cross sticker. Have an inflated balloon hidden behind you.

Teacher: Hi, Sprout! We're glad you're here today. Say hi to the girls and boys.

Sprout: Hi, everyone!

Teacher: I'd like you to meet *(name the children; if children are receptive, Sprout can give a little hug to each).* We're going to see you each Sunday and hear how much Jesus loves us.

Sprout: Each Sunday, that's cool! What else will we do?

Teacher: We'll make things . . .

Sprout: I saw everyone making a "God Made My Body" page. Good job, everybody!

Teacher: We'll hear about Jesus' love . . .

Sprout: Did you see what I wore today?

Teacher: Yes, I see you wore a cross [sticker]!

Sprout: That reminds me that Jesus loves you and me!

Teacher: That's right, Sprout! Jesus loves us so much that He died on the cross and then came alive again!

Sprout: I heard you singing so pretty. I like to sing songs.

Teacher: Will you sing a song with me?

Sprout: Oh, yes, I'd love to!

11, 12

Teacher: Let's all sing "God Is So Good" (CD, tracks 11, 12). We'll sing it a few times.

Sprout: That was great! Thanks for singing with me! God is so good to us—I'm glad He made our bodies so wonderfully. Watch what I can do! *(Sprout jumps high. Then he hides behind you. Then he hurries out from hiding. Finally, he bats a balloon over everyone's head.)*

Teacher: You can do so many things with your body, Sprout! We're glad. You can stay while we stand and sing a song about what our bodies can do.

6, 7

To help get the wiggles out, and to reinforce the lesson's focus, sing "I Can Stamp" (CD, tracks 6, 7), and do actions together. As time goes by, the children will join in the singing and movements. Afterwards, sit on the floor to hear today's Bible story.

Telling God's Word

Say **God is so good to us, just as we sang in the song. He made us —every part of our bodies—and He calls each of us His children.**

Show the Craft Page 1 from earlier. **God made [name each child]. God made our bodies so we can do so many different things!** (Use motions as you describe the following things.) **We can roll a ball, we can jump, we can wave our praise ribbons, we can stamp our feet we can pray—oh, so many things! God is so good to us!**

Stand and play a game with me. I'll say, "1-2-3, copy me!" Then you do what I do.

1-2-3, copy me! Jump up and down. **1-2-3, copy me!** Pat your head, then your knees. **1-2-3, copy me!** Turn slowly in a circle. **Look how God made our bodies to do so many things! 1-2-3, copy me!** Sit down.

Then show the God Made Adam and Eve Poster. Point to Adam and Eve in the picture. **These were the very first people God made. God made a man and named him Adam. Then He made a woman and called her Eve. God loved and cared for Adam and Eve. They were the first people that God made.**

Ask **Boys and girls, who did God make?** Encourage and prompt students to answer. Ask this a few times so they all can answer it.

Yes, God made Adam and Eve and God made you, and you, and you! You are a very special person. Have each child look into the large mirror. **Who do you see? That's [Kara]! God made you and loves you so much that He sent Jesus to be your Savior!**

Teacher Tip

Very young children need opportunities to move their bodies and get their wiggles out.

God made your mommy and daddy too. God made me and (add names of helpers). **I'm so glad God gave us our wonderful bodies!**

Wow! God loves you and me so much! We are all God's children because of Jesus! Point to the poster of Jesus.

Let's sing our Bible Words together. Play "God Cares for You" (CD, track 14) and encourage the children to sing with you as you play it several times. Then say the Bible Words with the children, clapping in rhythm on *God*, *cares*, and *you*. Then clap and say, God cares for me! **We're so happy that our God made us and cares for us.**

Now let's fold our hands and thank God for making our bodies.

Say very short echo-style prayers when praying with very young children. Pause at the * and repeat the words with them. Encourage parents to use this model at home too.

Pray **Thank You, God, for making our bodies.***
Thank You, God, for making the world.*
Thank You, God, for Jesus, our Savior.*
We know You love us.*
We know You care for us.*
We love You too.*
Amen.*

Say **We thank and praise God for His Word—for His Living Word, Jesus Christ. We want to tell others about Jesus, our Savior and Friend.** Point to the poster of Jesus.

Teacher Tip

Children and their parents may not have any experience praying. Routinely remind them to fold their hands. (We fold our hands simply to keep our hands still so that we can think about what we're saying to Jesus.)

Snack Time

Provide wet wipes for parents to clean their children's hands. Sing the echo prayer "Thank You, God, for This Food" (CD, track 15) as children fold their hands.

Say **God made our bodies. He gives us good food and drink to help our bodies grow and move.**

Provide water or juice to drink. Ask a child to give a napkin and paper plate to each person. Parents will need to help their children serve as helpers. Have parents give their children a few people-shaped cookies or crackers.

Or have parents squeeze spray-cheese onto a round cracker. Then children can place raisins on the cracker for the eyes, nose, and mouth.

Say **God made you and me. He made every part of our bodies. He made the whole world!**

Liturgy Link

As you move from prayer time to Snack Time, listen to the excerpt of "Thank the Lord and Sing His Praise" (CD, track 25) on the CD. Sing along a few times. Play the CD as children eat their snack and move from activity to activity. Remind parents and children to listen for this congregational response during worship.

3 We Live
10 minutes

Growing through God's Word—Parent Talk

A Two-Year-Old Develops Physically

While children eat their snacks explain that during these minutes, parents have the opportunity to share and discuss how children grow, learn, and what they can understand about God. Lead the parents through the following dialogue. If you have a helper, he or she may take the children to an area of the room to have a short playtime or to hear storybooks related to God's creation.

Read Psalm 139:13–16.

Say **Each child develops socially, emotionally, physically, intellectually, and spiritually according to God's timetable for him or her. Think about the unique characteristics your child has—their hair and eye color—their laugh—when they spoke their first words? If you have other children, you are already noticing differences from one child to the next. The psalmist speaks of being "fearfully and wonderfully made"—it's true! Take a moment to share some of the uniqueness of your child with another parent.**

Your child is truly a gift of God, yet, like you and I, your child is born sinful. We learn this in God's Word.

Read Psalm 51:5.

Say **We are all born sinful, and each of us needs to hear and know God's love and forgiveness. We're gathered here to hear God's forgiving and saving Word for us and our children. We come to church, God's house, to meet our Savior. We hear Him speak to us in the Bible readings and sermon and we feast at His table as He gives us His body and blood. Through His Word and Sacraments we are given the gifts of forgiveness, life, and salvation, and as a result, we can share the Gospel with these very young children, telling them that Jesus loves and forgives them. Tell your child frequently that God loves each of us so much that He sent His Son, Jesus, to die on the cross to take away our sins. He has made us His children through water and His Word in Holy Baptism.**

Discuss ways the children have grown physically since their conception. **God is our Creator. He knows us before we are even living beings. He makes our bodies and cares for us. What are some ways your children have grown physically?**

Ask **What are the limitations, if any, of the toddler age group?**

- Muscle control of large and small muscles has begun. Children may be clumsy, but like rough and tumble play and running.
- Fine motor skills are just beginning to develop. Since they were babies, they've picked up rattles, toys, and pieces of food, developing their grasping and hand-to-eye and hand-to-mouth movements. We do not expect toddlers to use pencils, crayons (other than chunky ones) or scissors. Most of the activities we do will require parental help and constant participation.
- Toddlers aren't comfortable in adult-size furniture. We do many activities because toddlers have short attention spans. We provide movement time because children often become restless. (Remind parents that they may need to take their restless little ones out of church, or leave the classroom for a short time and then return.)

Ask **What are things you can do to help your child's physical development?** Children like big boxes and tubes to crawl through! Toys

Teacher Tip

Encourage parents to use the Church's words when talking about God. This sacred vocabulary is learned like every day vocabulary from repeatedly hearing these words and being encouraged to speak them. As a child grows, he or she will also grow in understanding the meanings of the words.

need not be expensive, but make sure they are safe. Roll a ball, help your child jump over a chalk line, or place items from one box into another.

What things can you do to help your child's spiritual development? Pray with your child at mealtime, before bed, and throughout the day. Bring you child to church for worship, sit near the front so they can see what is going on. Speak often of Jesus, their Savior and Friend!

Say **Jesus is with us, helping us play, pray, share, forgive, and have fun together.**

11, 12

Move back to your Singing Circle area. Play or hum "God Is So Good" (CD, tracks 11, 12).

Say **We're in our Singing Circle again, ready to say good-bye.**

Teacher Tip
You might provide a folder labeled "Parents & Twos Family Pages" and give it to each family after the first class.

4 Closing
10 minutes

Songs and Prayers

Ask **Do you remember our Bible, God's Word?** Show the Toddler Bible you use during storytelling. **Today we heard how God made each one of us and gave us our bodies. Let's do this action rhyme together:**

Say
God made you, *(Point to each child.)*
God made me! *(Point to yourself.)*
God loves you, *(Point to each child.)*
God loves me! *(Point to yourself.)*
God made everything! *(Extend arms wide.)*
Thank You, God! *(Extend arms upward.)*

Teacher Tip
It's important to say a personal good-bye to each child and his or her parent(s). Be at each child's eye level as you say, **God made you, [Jesse]! God cares for you!**

Ask **Who made our bodies? That's right, God made us! Let's fold our hands and thank God for making each of us. You can say the prayer words after I say the words.**

Pray
Dear God,*
Thank You for making (name each child).*
Thank You for Jesus, our Savior and Friend*
You love us so much!*
We love You!*
Amen.*

20

Sing "Now It's Time to Say Good-bye" (CD, track 20)

Take Homes

Family Page 1—Encourage parents to review, sing, and pray with their children. Remind them to save their Family Pages in a sturdy folder for future reference.

Craft Page 1

Bible Story Booklet—Encourage parents to review the pages and concepts with their children as they speak about God as our Maker and Jesus as our Savior.

Lesson 2

God Made the World—God Made My Eyes

Genesis 2

Key Point

God is so good. God made my eyes to see everything in God's world.

Connections

Bible Words
[God] cares for you. 1 Peter 5:7

Faith Words
God, Jesus, maker

Catechism
Apostles' Creed: First Article
I believe in God the Father Almighty, Maker of heaven and earth.

Liturgy
Thank the Lord and sing His praise; tell everyone what he has done.

Hymn
All Creatures of Our God and King (*Lutheran Worship* 436)

Materials Needed

1 Opening

Teacher Tools
- Nametags
- Family Info Page
- CD
- Craft Page 2: God Made My Eyes

Other Supplies
- See "To Prepare" instructions for each Activity Center
- Rhythm ribbons or scarves

2 God Speaks

Teacher Tools
- CD
- Sprout Puppet
- God Made My Eyes to See Poster
- God Made Adam and Eve Poster

Other Supplies
- Poster of Jesus
- Flowers for Sprout
- Toddler Bible
- Large mirror

3 We Live

Teacher Tools
- Bible

4 Closing

Teacher Tools
- Family Page 2

Other Supplies
- Toddler Bible

1 Opening
30 minutes

Welcome

Smile and say hello, using each child and parent's name as they enter the room. Remind them to wear a nametag and point them to the day's focus: "God Made My Eyes to See." Ask parents to choose an activity to begin with their children, and as they do so, focus on God's gift of eyes and eyesight in His wonderful world.

Activity Centers

Water

To Prepare: Watercolors or watercolor markers.

Cover a table with a vinyl tablecloth and place a plastic pan with about 3 inches of water on the tablecloth. Provide measuring cups, small funnels, and plastic scoops. Have a towel or paper towels at this area. Before class, swish watercolor paint or watercolor markers through the water to add a color.

Say **It's fun to pour water from cup to cup. What do you see different about the water today? What part of your body helps you to see that the water is different? What color is the water today? I'm so glad God gave us eyes so we can see everything in the world He made!**

We can see the water when Pastor baptizes a baby!

Art

To Prepare: Craft Page 2: God Made My Eyes; a variety of colorful stickers; construction paper.

Have parents help children scribble-color the "God Made My Eyes" page. As they color, talk about the many things that our eyes can see in God's world.

Say **Our eyes are God's gifts to us. They allow us to see the things God has made in His world. Add stickers showing a variety of people, animals, flowers, foods, pets, and a cross to remind us of our Savior, Jesus, who took all our sins away.**

Give each child a background paper and a zipper bag of a variety of colorful stickers. Ask parents to print their children's names in a corner of the paper.

Say **Allow your child to choose and place the stickers on the paper. Their choices, and the process of seeing the colors, and attaching the stickers are all more important than what the finished product looks like. Children will gradually learn color names as you talk about them during your everyday activities.**

Look at the pretty, yellow puppy! See the bright pink flower! We thank God for making our eyes to see all the beautiful things He makes for us. What a wonderful gift our eyesight is from God!

Here is a cross sticker. It reminds us that God sent Jesus to die on the cross and take all our sins away. Jesus came alive, and He is our Savior and Friend.

Play Dough

To Prepare: Set out various colors of play dough, child-size rolling pins, and a variety of cookie cutter shapes.

Say **What part of our body do we use to see the play dough? To see the cookie cutters? Thank You, God, for our eyes.**

Can you roll your play dough into a long snake? Our eyes help us see the snake.

Roll your play dough into a ball. What color is your ball? Can you make a cross shape? I'm glad we have eyes to see!

Discovery

To Prepare: Trays for items; nature items safe for children to touch—shells, rocks, leaves, flowers, feathers, bark, twigs; cardboard tissue tube "binoculars"; colorful cellophane; rubber bands; a magnifying glass; View-Master and slide wheel; a hand-held mirror.

Place a variety of nature items on one or two cookie sheets or trays.

Say **God made many things for us to enjoy in His world!**

Show children how to look through the cardboard tube binoculars (or real binoculars if you have them) to see items in the room.

Say **Do you see the cross? Look for the picture of Jesus. Thank You, Jesus, for dying on the cross for us. Thank You for coming alive again! Do you see the Bible? Thank You, Jesus, for giving us Your holy Word. See the flowers at our worship center. Do you see the cloth on our altar? What color is it?**

Attach a square of colored cellophane with a rubber band to one end of a cardboard tube. Have children look through the tube to see items in the room.

Use the Growing in Christ View-Master with the slides of Bible story art.

Say **See the Bible story pictures in the View-Master? God cares for His people! We thank God for the gift of our eyes and being able to see things.**

Hold a mirror so that a child can see himself or herself.

Say **Who do you see in the mirror? YOU! Our eyes help us see ourselves.**

Hang the poster "God Made My Eyes to See" near this Activity Center.

Say **Can you see the church and point to it? Point to the cross. Now find the pastor. God made our eyes to see all these things!**

What do you see with your eyes? Thank You, God, for our eyes to see our friends today, to see the books and fun activities, to see the pictures on our posters, and so much more in Your world.

Teacher Tip

You can order the Growing in Christ View-Master and Bible story picture wheels from CPH, item number: 41-1029.

Pretend

To Prepare: Baby dolls; kitchen play items; blocks; trucks and cars.

Encourage children to play with the toys in an active area of your room.

Say **We're so glad God made our eyes to see. Look at your baby doll. What color eyes does he have? What else can you see on your doll? Can you see his ears?**

Use your eyes to find a green car, a red truck, a police car, a fire engine, a truck with big wheels.

Can you find the play food? Use your eyes to help you put the food onto a plate. Thank You, God, for making our eyes to see! Use your eyes to give Mommy or Daddy the breakfast you made. How did you find Mommy or Daddy? You used your eyes!

Books and Puzzles

Simple shape and color puzzles; peg puzzles of people of all ages

Picture and board books about God's creation

The Apostles' Creed—Follow and Do by Joni Walker, CPH (56-2336)

Why I Love You, God by Michelle Medlock Adams, CPH (56-2165)

This Is the World That God Made by Martha Streufert Jander, CPH (54-0080)

Things I See in Church, by Julie Stiegemeyer, CPH (56-2227)

Transition

Remind families a few minutes before it's time to put away activities. Then sing "Let's Clean Up" (CD, tracks 1, 2) and move to the Singing Circle area. Play "Thank the Lord and Sing His Praise" and "1 Peter 5:7" (CD, tracks 25, 21) as families move from cleaning up to gathering to sing.

Singing Circle

Provide colorful praise ribbons or scarves for children to wave, and encourage them to move and dance to the music. Remember to repeat songs from past weeks.

Sing

First Article Song

Morning Prayer Song

1 Peter 5:7

All Creatures of Our God and King

Good Morning to You

Happy Birthday to You and **God Made Me His Child** to celebrate special occasions.

I Can Stamp (Add verses to go with each lesson.)

Jesus Loves the Little Ones

He's Got the Whole World in His Hands (Variation: "He's Got the Girls and the Boys in His Hands," etc.)

God Is So Good (Variation: "God made my eyes . . .)

2 God Speaks
10 minutes

Come to the Worship Center

Have children sit in front of the altar to hear today's Bible story. Have a cloth strip in the color appropriate for the Church Year on the altar. Sing or hum "God Is So Good" or "Thank the Lord and Sing His Praise" (CD, tracks 11, 25) as everyone gathers. Thank everyone for coming so nicely and for being ready to listen. Do the action rhyme "Open Them, Close Them" (CD, track 13) to help children learn to keep their hands in their laps and to focus on listening.

Say **In the name of the Father and of the Son and of the Holy Spirit. Amen.** Make the sign of the cross as you say this and invite the children to repeat these holy words with you.

Introducing God's Word

Sprout wears a brightly colored flower pinned to his shoulder.

Sprout: Hi, everyone! See what I have today! See my pretty flower!

Teacher: Your flower is beautiful, Sprout. I see that it's a very bright [color name]!

Sprout: God is so good. He made my flower. Mommy picked it out of her garden for me to wear today.

Teacher: I'm glad you're wearing it so that we can all see how pretty it is.

Sprout: God makes lots of pretty flowers. Orange ones, yellow ones, red ones, and even blue flowers! Like the ones here at our worship center!

Teacher: And I'm so glad we can see all those colors and flowers, Sprout.

Sprout: I just wanted to show you and all the boys and girls my flower. It makes me happy to see pretty things.

Teacher: Seeing pretty flowers and other things in God's world makes us all happy. We're glad God made our eyes so we can see so much every day!

Sprout: God sure did a good job when He made our eyes to see!

Teacher: Yes, He did, Sprout! Our eyes are God's gift to us to see His world. We can sing a song about our eyes. Will you sing it with us?

Sprout: Oh, yes, I'd love to!

Teacher: Let's sing "God Is So Good." We'll add the verse "God made my eyes." *(CD, track 12; repeat the song a few times.)*

Sprout: That was fun! God is so good to us—I'm glad He made our eyes to see!

Teacher: You can stay and sing another song with us, Sprout. We'll stand and do the actions too.

To help get wiggles out, sing "I Can Stamp" (CD, track 7) and do actions together. Then sit on the floor to continue with today's Bible story.

Telling God's Word

Say **God is so good to us. He made our eyes to see so many things!**

Show the God Made My Eyes to See Poster. Point to each item as you say its name. Then have children and parents repeat what you say.

Say **I see the altar.** *(Echo)*
Thank You, God, for my eyes. *(Echo)*
I see the cross. *(Echo)*
Thank You, God, for my eyes. *(Echo)*

I see the pastor. *(Echo)*
Thank You, God, for my eyes. *(Echo)*

Have each child look into the big mirror. **Who do you see? That's [Joseph]! God made your eyes to see! God cares for you!**

Show the God Made Adam and Eve Poster. **God gave Adam and Eve eyes to see. Look at some of the things they saw with their eyes. What beautiful trees and flowers! What animals did they see? God gave us eyes to see all that He made.**

14

Point to the poster of Jesus. **Let's say our Bible Words together.** Hold the Bible open as you say the words. **God cares for you!** As you say the Bible Words a few times, clap on *God*, *cares*, and *you*. Then play the Bible Words Song, "God Cares for you," on the CD (track 14).

Now let's pray and thank God for making our eyes to see.

Have children repeat the words of the prayer after you. Pause at the * and repeat the words with them.

Teacher Tip
Remind everyone to fold their hands, simply to keep our hands still so we can think about what we're saying to God, our maker.

Pray **Thank You, God, for making our eyes.***
Thank You, God, for helping us to see Jesus.*
Thank You for making the world!*
We know You love us.*
We love You too.*
Amen.*

Say **We thank and praise God for His Word—for His Living Word, Jesus Christ, and want to tell others about Jesus!** Point to the poster of Jesus.

Snack Time

15

Provide wet wipes for parents to clean the children's hands. Sing the echo prayer "Thank You, God, for This Food" (CD, track 15) as children fold their hands.

Say **We're glad we can see our snacks today! Thank You, God, for the gift of our eyes.**

Provide water or juice to drink. Ask a child to give a napkin and paper plate to each person. Parents will need to help their children serve as helpers.

Have parents give their children pieces of the snacks you've chosen for today.

Option: Ask parents to squeeze cheese onto a round cracker. Then, with parents' help, children can place raisins on the cracker for the eyes, nose, and mouth.

Say **God has made you and me. He made the whole world!**

Liturgy Link
Listen to "Thank the Lord and Sing His Praise" on the CD (track 25). Sing along a few times. Remind parents and children to listen for this congregational response during worship.

3 We Live
10 minutes

Growing through God's Word—Parent Talk

A Two-Year-Old Develops Emotionally

While children eat their snacks, lead the parents through the following dialogue and questions. If you have a team leader, he or she may take the children to an area of the room to have a short playtime or to hear additional storybooks related to God's creation.

Say **Today, we learned about how God makes our eyes so that we can see. In Hebrews 12:22, St. Paul tells us to "Fix our eyes on Jesus." How do you help your little one "see" Jesus? Speak of going to church as going to God's house, where we see Jesus. Tell your child that we "see" Jesus in the water of Baptism and as the pastor speaks Jesus' Word to us. We also "see" Him when we go up to the altar for Communion, Jesus' special meal. Start now, planting these thoughts and images in your child's mind. Though they are abstract concepts, your child will accept them because they trust you, and their understanding of these concepts will come as they grow in their faith.**

Read Psalm 139:13–16.

Say **God has made each one of us in His image. Because of sin, we are separated from our heavenly Father and can't help ourselves. In His great love for us, God gave Jesus to break down sin's barrier through His death and resurrection! He made us, cares for us, and keeps us in His family through the Word and water of Baptism.** Have parents share ways that they reinforce God's love and forgiveness for their children.

God created us with all our emotions. What are some of those emotions? By the time we're adults, we've learned to control our emotions for the most part. Having emotions and self-control are a major part of growing and maturing!

Young children's emotions lie on the surface. They let you know how they feel all the time. Which emotions do you recognize your child having? Allow parents to share.

Toddlers are naturally self-centered, seeing everything from their own viewpoint. They haven't yet learned to see things from others' viewpoints. They can't understand the reasons behind knowing right from wrong yet, but they can experience God's love for us in Jesus as we hug and love them and let them know how much we care about them. Think of a situation that illustrates the self-centeredness of your two-year-old. (Allow parents to share.)

In your vocation as parents you need to help your child avoid seeing things that are not God pleasing. Monitor what your child views on TV, in magazines, as well as other visual images in your home.

What are things you can do to help your child's emotional development?

- Help your child express emotions by teaching words to describe them: "I'm angry that Kristen took my book away"; "I'm excited that Grandpa is coming to visit."
- Give your child opportunities to play with other children. Expect them to play side by side. Encourage the sharing of toys.
- Provide a hug, a time of rocking, or individual attention when your child shows that he needs his emotions recognized and affirmed.

- Bring your child to worship. Sit near the front so she can see and hear well. Express your joy at being able to praise and thank God.

11, 25

Move back to your Singing Circle area. Play or hum "God Is So Good" or "Thank the Lord and Sing His Praise" (CD, tracks 11, 25).

Say **Let's get ready to say good-bye to each other.**

4 Closing
10 minutes

Songs and Prayers

Ask **Do you remember our Bible, God's Word?** Show the Toddler Bible you use during storytelling. **Today we heard how God made our eyes for us to see. Let's do this action rhyme together:**

God made you, *(Point to each child.)*
God made me! *(Point to yourself.)*
God loves you, *(Point to each child.)*
God loves me! *(Point to yourself.)*
God made your eyes to see! *(Point to children's eyes.)*
God made my eyes to see! *(Point to your eyes.)*
God loves you, *(Point to each child.)*
God loves me! *(Point to yourself.)*

Say **Who has made our eyes? That's right, God made our eyes! He made the whole world! Let's fold our hands and thank God for making our eyes to see. You can say the prayer words after I say the words.**

Pray **Dear God,***
Thank You for making my eyes.*
Thank You for making the world!*
Thank You for helping us see.*
Thank You for Jesus, our Savior and Friend*
You love us so much!*
We love You too!*
Amen.*

20

Sing "Now It's Time to Say Good-bye" (CD, track 20)

Say Good-bye

Say **Look for things to see with your eyes in church and at home.**

Take Homes

Family Page 2—Encourage parents to review today's Bible lesson, sing, and pray with their children.

Craft Page 2

Bible Story Booklet for families who missed the previous class. Encourage all parents to review the pages and concepts with their children as they speak about Jesus and His love and care for all of God's creation.

Teacher Tip

Remember to say a personal good-bye to each child and his or her parent(s).

Lesson 3

God Made the World—God Made My Ears

Genesis 2

Kcy Point

God is so good. God made my ears to hear His Word and all the sounds in His wonderful world.

Connections

Bible Words
[God] cares for you. 1 Peter 5:7

Faith Words
God, Jesus, maker

Catechism
Apostles' Creed: First Article
I believe in God the Father Almighty, Maker of heaven and earth.

Liturgy
Thank the Lord and sing His praise; tell everyone what He has done.

Hymn
All Creatures of Our God and King (*Lutheran Worship* 436)

Materials Needed

1 Opening

Teacher Tools
- Nametags
- Teacher CD
- God Made My Ears to Hear Poster

Other Supplies
- See "To Prepare" instructions for each Activity Center
- Maracas made at art center
- Rhythm ribbons and scarves

2 God Speaks

Teacher Tools
- Teacher CD
- Sprout Puppet
- God Made Adam and Eve Poster

Other Supplies
- Poster of Jesus
- Toddler Bible
- Large mirror

3 We Live

Teacher Tools
- Bible

4 Closing

Teacher Tools
- Family Page 3

Other Supplies
- Toddler Bible

1 Opening
30 minutes

Welcome

Say hello using each child and parent's name as they enter the room. Remind them to wear a nametag, and point them to the day's focus: "God Made My Ears to Hear." Direct parents to choose an activity to begin with their children, and as they do so, focus on God's gift of ears and hearing.

Activity Centers

Water

To Prepare: Pan; measuring cups; small funnels; plastic scoops; small wire whisks; egg beater; plastic fork.

Cover a table with a vinyl tablecloth and place a plastic pan holding about 3 inches of water on the tablecloth. Provide measuring cups, small funnels, and plastic scoops. Add items that make noise today—egg beater, whisks, a fork. Have a towel or paper towels at this area.

Say **It's fun to pour water and use tools to make noise in the water. What sound do you hear when you beat the water? Use the fork to go back and forth. Can you make swishing sounds with the whisk? Pastor poured water over you when you were Baptized, he poured it over you three times, in the name of the Father and of the Son and of the Holy Spirit. We thank God for making our ears so we can hear!**

Art

To Prepare: Craft Page 3: God Made My Ears; a variety of colorful stickers; construction paper circles cut to fit small margarine tub lids; craft glue; rice.

Have families color and talk about the Craft Page 3. Add happy face stickers or stickers of animals and people.

Ask **What does God help us hear in His great world? Thank You, God, for the gift of our ears!**

Give each family a colorful, precut paper circle and a few colorful stickers.

Say **Decorate your circle with the stickers.** Talk about how wonderful God is to make all the pretty things in our world and to give us ears to hear the sounds around us. **Our ears are God's gift so we can hear sounds.**

Give each family a small margarine tub and lid. **Glue your circle decoration to the top of the plastic lid. After you add a scoop of rice to the tub, use the craft glue to secure the lid to the container. Shake your maraca and hear the sounds of the rice. We'll let the maracas dry and use them later as we sing and praise God.**

Play Dough

Provide various colors of play dough, child-size rolling pins, and a variety of cookie cutters (people and animal shapes).

Liturgy Link

Adam and Eve were created in God's image, righteous and holy, doing His will. This image was lost at the fall into sin. Thus, when we say the Confession in church, we acknowledge that we are by nature sinful and unclean. In Christians, God has begun to rebuild His image, but only in heaven will it be fully restored. So, we also pray in the Confession, "Forgive us, renew us, and lead us, so that we may delight in Your will and walk in Your ways" (*LW*, p. 158).

Ask **What part of our body do we use to hear Mommy and Daddy talk to us? To hear the cow moo? What sound do you hear when you pound the play dough? When you cut it?**

Thank You, God, for making our ears so we can hear each other!

Discovery

To Prepare: God Made My Ears to Hear Poster; objects to demonstrate sounds—wind-up clock, bell, drum, xylophone, whistle, baby rattle, noisy toys.

Place a variety of items appropriate for children to handle as they discover the sounds they make. Also include a Bible.

Say **Thank You, God, for the gift of our ears and our hearing.**

Play a listening game. Use an object to make a noise behind you (crumple paper; shake a rattle; tap spoons together). Have families guess what made that sound.

Hang the God Made My Ears to Hear Poster near this Activity Center.

Say **Can you point to the bell? What sound does the bell make? The water? What does a kitty say? A doggy? A lion?**

Thank You, God, for our ears that hear.

If you have a clock that chirps birds' songs, listen to those with the children. Show them the birds and let them hear the different bird songs.

Say **God made a wonderful world, full of beautiful bird sounds and other sounds for us to enjoy!**

Have a Bible on the table, allow the children to hold it.

Ask **How do we hear the Bible? We hear God's Word when our pastor, teacher, and parents read it to us. We hear that Jesus saves and loves us!**

Pretend

To Prepare: Hammer and wood blocks; pound-a-peg toys; popcorn maker; pull-toys; play vacuum cleaner; lawn mower; other toys that make sounds.

As children play with the items, ask them what sounds they hear.

Say **We're so glad God made our ears to hear. Thank You, God!**

Have parents make sounds we hear in everyday life such as a siren, a phone ring, a door knock, a book closing, spoons tapping together.

Ask **What did you hear?**

26–30

Play the church sounds from the Teacher CD (tracks 26–30).

Ask **Where do we hear these sounds?**

Books and Puzzles

Simple shape and color puzzles; peg puzzles of people of all ages

Picture and board books about God's creation

Apostles' Creed—Follow and Do by Joni Walker, CPH (56-2336)

Things I Hear in Church by Julie Stiegemeyer, CPH (56-2203)

Transition

Sing "Let's Clean Up" (CD, tracks 1, 2) and move to the Singing Circle. Play "Thank the Lord and Sing His Praise" (CD, track 25) as everyone gathers.

Singing Circle

Provide colorful praise ribbons or scarves for children to wave. Encourage them to move and dance to the music.

Sing **First Article Song**

Morning Prayer Song

1 Peter 5:7

All Creatures of Our God and King

Good Morning to You

Happy Birthday to You and **God Made Me His Child** to celebrate special occasions.

I Can Stamp (Add verses to go with each lesson, such as "I can listen with my ears . . . God gave me these ears.")

Jesus Loves the Little Ones

He's Got the Whole World in His Hands (Variation: "He's Got the Girls and the Boys in His Hands" and "He's Got the Tiny Little Babies in His Hands.")

God Is So Good (Variation: "God Made My Ears")

Teacher Tip

Very young children need the opportunities to move their bodies and get their wiggles out.

2 God Speaks

10 minutes

Come to the Worship Center

Have children sit on a special rug or quilt to get ready to hear today's Bible story. Sing or hum "God Is So Good" or "1 Peter 5:7" (CD, tracks 11 or 21 as everyone gathers. Thank everyone for coming so nicely and for being ready to listen. Do the action rhyme "Open Them, Close Them" (CD, track 13) to teach the children to keep their hands in their laps and to listen.

Say **In the name of the Father and of the Son and of the Holy Spirit. Amen.** Make the sign of the cross as you say this and invite the children to repeat these holy words with you.

Introducing God's Word

Sprout comes out singing "God Made My Ears, He's So Good to Me" and moving to the rhythm.

Teacher: We hear you singing a happy song, Sprout!

Sprout: God is so good. He made my ears so I can hear. I heard all of you singing too!

Teacher: Yes, we sang and praised God. Did you hear our instruments too?

Sprout: Oh, yes! I like to hear those sounds!

Teacher: What other sounds have you heard today, Sprout?

Sprout: I heard birds singing. Did you, girls and boys?

Teacher: Did anyone hear the organ music in church?

Sprout: Yes! It's beautiful! I heard the bell ring when church started too.

Teacher: Did you hear people say "Good morning" to each other?

Sprout: Oh, yes! Everyone is happy to see each other.

Teacher: Boys and girls, did you hear the pastor speak God's Word?

It's great to have ears that can hear God's Word! Let's play a listening game. You can play too, Sprout. We'll listen to sounds on the CD and guess what each sound is. (*Play a few seconds of the Church Sounds from the Teacher CD [tracks 26–30] and allow time for families to guess each sound. Allow general answers like: "That's the pastor," "Those are bells," or "That's the congregation singing."*)

Sprout: That was fun! You really used your listening ears!

Teacher: Everyone listened so well. Our God is so good to us—I'm glad He made our ears to hear so well.

Sprout: Oh, I hear someone calling me! I have to go now. I'll see you next time. Keep using your ears to listen! They are God's gift to you!

To help get wiggles out and to reinforce the lesson's focus, sing "I Can Stamp" (CD, tracks 6, 7) and do actions together. Add the lyrics for today: "I can listen with my ears . . . God gave me these ears." Then sit on the floor again to continue with today's Bible story.

Telling God's Word

Say **God is so good to us. He made our ears to hear so many sounds in His world!**

Show the God Made My Ears to Hear Poster. Point to each item as you say its name. Then have children and parents repeat what you say, and add the thank-you statement.

Say **I hear the bells ring.** *(Echo)*
Thank You, God, for my ears! *(Echo)*
I hear the people sing. *(Echo)*
Thank You, God, for my ears! *(Echo)*
I hear the pastor pray. *(Echo)*
Thank You, God, for my ears! *(Echo)*

Say Have each child look into the big mirror. **Who do you see? That's [Caroline]! Point to your ears. God made your ears! God cares for you so much!**

Show the God Made Adam and Eve Poster. **God gave the first people, Adam and Eve, ears to hear in the world that He made. What are some of the things they heard in the beautiful garden?**

Point to the poster of Jesus. **Let's say our Bible Words together.** Open the Bible as if to read from it. **God cares for you!** Say the words and clap the rhythm two or three times. **We're so glad that we can hear stories of Jesus and His love and hear songs and hymns and Bible Words.** Then sing "1 Peter 5:7" together (CD, track 21).

Let's fold our hands and thank God for making our ears to hear.

Teacher Tip

Fold hands, teaching families that when we keep our hands still, we can think about what we're saying to Jesus.

Have children repeat the words of the prayer after you. Pause at * and repeat the words with them. Encourage parents to use this model.

Pray **Thank You, God, for making our ears.***
Thank You for making the whole world.*
Thank You, God, for your Word, the Bible,*
Thank You that we can hear about Jesus, our Savior.*
We know You love us.*
We love You too.*
Amen.*

Snack Time

Provide wet wipes for parents to clean the children's hands. Sing the echo prayer "Thank You, God, for This Food" (CD, track 15) as children fold their hands.

Say **We're glad God helps us hear our snack song and all the crunchy snacks we have today!**

Provide water or juice to drink. Ask a child to give a napkin and paper plate to each person. Parents will need to help their children serve as helpers. Have parents give their children portions of the crunchy snacks.

Ask **What sound do you hear when you drink? When you chew? When you swallow? Thanks, God, for the gift of our ears!**

Liturgy Link

Listen to "Thank the Lord and Sing His Praise" on the CD (CD, track 25). Sing along a few times. Remind parents and children to listen for this congregational response during worship. Talk about how we use our ears in church to hear God's Word for us.

3 We Live
10 minutes

Growing through God's Word—Parent Talk

A Two-Year-Old Develops Spiritually

Lead the parents through the following dialogue and questions. If you have a team leader, he or she may take the children to an area of the room to have a short playtime or to hear storybooks related to God's creation.

Say **After Adam and Eve sinned the first time in the Garden of Eden, all people have been born in sin, it is part of our human nature. Even newborn babies are born sinful and are separated from God by sin.**

Read Psalm 51:5 and Romans 3:23.

Say **It's sometimes hard to think that our precious little child is a sinner. Think back to when your child was a newborn. What examples can you give that show sinfulness in his or her life?** Selfishness and greed can be seen even in young children. They may demand things and get upset when they don't get them. Talk about children's true needs and the parents' responsibilities to fill them.

We believe in original sin and its effects on each of us as well as its effects upon our world. Sickness is a result of sin in our world. Death is a result of sin. Romans 6:23 tells us that "the wages of sin is death, but the free gift of God is eternal life in Christ Jesus our Lord!" This is why we baptize infants. They, like us, are sinners in need of a Savior. In His Word, you and your child can read and hear about our loving Father who sent His Son, Jesus, to suffer and die for us, granting forgiveness for all our sins. When Jesus died on the cross, He took away the sins of all. God's grace is free! God's grace and forgiveness is learned through you as you speak God's Word and share the forgiveness He gave you.

Ask parents to share a time in their lives when God's grace became real to them. **Who told you the Gospel message? How is your life different knowing and believing that Jesus has taken your sins to His cross?** Be prepared to share your experience if no one volunteers.

What ways do you model forgiveness for your child? We hug, say, "I love you," say, "I forgive you" and also say, "Please forgive me" as we model Christ's forgiveness for us all. **It is important for each of us to HEAR these words. As your child hears them, he or she will also learn to speak them to the people in his or her life.**

In a beautiful and most direct way, God comes to us in His Word, preached and read to us, and in His Sacraments of Baptism and the Lord's Supper, given to us in the worship service. It is important for both you and your child to come to God's house often to hear and receive these means of grace!

Our loving God wants ALL people to be His children. God brings His children into His family through Baptism—by water and His Word. Faith begins at the baptismal font and the Holy Spirit becomes alive in your children's hearts, working faith through God's Word. Encourage parents to show their children photos and mementos of Baptism and to celebrate Baptism anniversaries by lighting a candle and singing a special song. If families have adults and children who are not yet baptized, encourage them to talk with you and your pastor about Baptism. Make your pastor aware of these people.

Let's read Deuteronomy 6:6–8 and find out what God says about parents' responsibilities to nurture new faith in babies and toddlers. Discuss the importance of reading, teaching, and listening to God's Word, having family devotions daily, praying, singing, and attending worship together.

Remember that your child learns through concrete, hands-on experiences—not through abstract thinking. Through the work of the Holy Spirit, your child learns to trust God as he or she trusts you. They learn to love God as they see you worship. They learn through you by living in joy, acceptance, hope, forgiveness, kindness, love, and sharing experiences.

11, 25

Move to your Singing Circle area. Sing "God Is So Good" or "Thank the Lord and Sing His Praise" (CD, tracks 11 or 25) while everyone comes together.

Say **We're in our Singing Circle again. Let's get ready to say good-bye.**

4 Closing
10 minutes

Songs and Prayers

Ask Show the Toddler Bible you use during storytelling. **Today, we listened so well with our ears! We heard how God made our ears for us to hear. Let's do this action rhyme together:**

God made you, *(Point to each child.)*
God made me! *(Point to yourself.)*
God made your ears to hear! *(Point to children's eyes.)*
God made my ears to hear! *(Point to your eyes.)*
I can hear God's Word! *(Point to the Bible.)*
God loves you, *(Point to each child.)*
God loves me! *(Point to yourself.)*

Say **Who has made our ears? That's right, God made our ears! He made the whole world! Let's fold our hands and thank God for making our ears to hear so well. God gives us ears to hear that Jesus is our Savior in His Word. God gives us so many sounds to hear in His world. You can hear the prayer words with your ears, and then say the prayer words after I say them.**

Pray **Dear God,***
Thank You for making my ears.*
Thank You for helping me hear.*
Thank You for Your Word that I can hear*
Thank You that I can hear about Jesus, my Savior.*
You love us so much!*
We love You too!*
Amen.*

20 **Sing** "Now It's Time to Say Good-bye" (CD, track 20)

Say Good-bye

Say a personal good-bye to each child and his or her parent(s).

Say **Listen for sounds! Tell Mommy or Daddy the sounds you hear today on your way home!**

Take Homes

Family Page 3—Encourage parents to review today's Bible lesson, sing and pray with their children.

Child's Maraca

Craft Page 3

Bible Story Booklet for families who missed previous classes. Encourage all parents to review the pages and concepts with their children as they hear about Jesus and His love and care for all God's creation.

Lesson 4

God Made the World—God Made My Nose

Genesis 2

Key Point

God is so good. God made my nose to smell wonderful scents in His world.

Connections

Bible Words
[God] cares for you. 1 Peter 5:7

Faith Words
God, Jesus, maker

Catechism
Apostles' Creed: First Article
I believe in God the Father Almighty, Maker of heaven and earth.

Liturgy
Thank the Lord and sing His praise; tell everyone what He has done.

Hymn
All Creatures of Our God and King (*Lutheran Worship* 436)

Materials Needed

1 Opening

Teacher Tools
- Nametags
- Teacher CD
- God Made My Nose to Smell Poster
- Craft Page 4: God Made My Nose

Other Supplies
- See "To Prepare" instructions for each Activity Center
- Rhythm instruments

2 God Speaks

Teacher Tools
- Teacher CD
- Sprout Puppet
- God Made Adam and Eve Poster

Other Supplies
- Fresh orange
- Poster of Jesus
- Bouquet of flowers (1 flower per child)—real or scented silk flowers
- Vase for flowers
- Toddler Bible
- Large mirror

3 We Live

Teacher Tools
- Bible

4 Closing

Teacher Tools
- Sprout puppet
- Family Page 4

Other Supplies
- Toddler Bible

1 Opening
30 minutes

Welcome

Warmly welcome the families and direct them to the day's focus: "God Made My Nose to Smell."

Say **Choose an activity to begin with your child as you focus on God's gift of our noses and the ability to smell things in His world.**

Activity Centers

Water

To Prepare: Vanilla, almond, or peppermint extract or scented oils; small sponge.

Add scented oil to the water pan today. Provide small sponges for children to squeeze in the water and smell.

Say **Smell the water. Do you like the [peppermint] smell? We thank God for making our noses and helping us to smell things!**

Art

To Prepare: Craft Page 4: God Made My Nose; stickers—flowers, nature items, food items, animals; cookie sheet or 9 × 13-inch pan; scented hand lotion; dark construction paper; menthol-scented shaving cream.

Using Craft Page 4, have families color and talk about things in God's world that we can smell. Add stickers of flowers, animals, and food items.

Say **Thanks, God, for the gift of our noses and our ability to smell things in Your world!**

Place about one tablespoon of scented hand/body lotion on the cookie sheet or in the baking pan before each child's activity.

Say **Use your fingers to paint a picture in the lotion. Can you smell the lotion? What does it smell like? Is it a good smell? God gave us our noses to smell things in His world.**

As each child creates a lotion picture, one at a time, gently press a piece of dark construction paper onto the lotion. Then carefully lift the paper and hang or store it to dry.

Encourage children to share the lotion on their hands with their moms and dads.

Have children finger paint with shaving cream on a tabletop. Smell the scent. Thank God for noses that can smell! Have paper towels or wet wipes for cleaning.

Play Dough

To Prepare: Provide two different batches of scented play dough by adding oil of peppermint, almond, or vanilla to it; child-size rolling pins; cookie cutters of people, flowers, and animals.

Say **What does this play dough smell like? Do you like this smell?**

Which smell do you like best? We can smell the play dough because God gave us noses to smell things in His world.

Have children use the rolling pins and cookie cutters to create cookies to "bake" at the pretend area.

Discovery

To Prepare: God Made My Nose to Smell Poster; organic items for children to smell—flowers, pine needles, cinnamon sticks, orange slices, lemon slices, chocolate shavings, leaves, grass, soil, apple slices; scented cotton balls—lemon, perfume fragrance, household cleanser, coffee, vanilla, almond, peppermint, nail polish remover, hand/body lotion; paper plates, candle, matches, and a flower.

Scent cotton balls with various fragrances. Put each cotton ball on a separate paper plate. Place a variety of organic items appropriate for children to handle as they discover the scents and fragrances.

Say **God made wonderful smells for you to enjoy. Do you like this smell? Which smell is your favorite?**

Ask **What does this smell like? Do you like this smell? God gives us our noses to smell things in His world.**

Point to the God Made My Nose to Smell Poster and have children tell which smell(s) they like.

Ask **What can we smell in God's house, the church?** Light a candle and blow it out, let the children smell the smoke. Hold up a fresh flower and let children smell it.

Pretend

To Prepare: Bowls; spoons; spatulas; cookie sheets; pots and pans.

Say **Let's make pretend cookies today. What kind are you making? What do your cookies smell like?**

Have parents pretend to cook dinner with the children using the pots, pans, spoons, and any play kitchen tools available.

Say **Do you smell the spaghetti sauce cooking? Yum, I smell your brownies baking! Let's stir the pan of cinnamon oatmeal now. God is so good to give us noses that can smell wonderful things!**

Books and Puzzles

Simple shape and color puzzles; peg puzzles of people of all ages

Picture and board books about God's creation

Apostles' Creed—Follow and Do by Joni Walker, CPH (56-2336)

Why I Love You, God by Michelle Medlock Adams, CPH (56-2165)

Transition

Sing "Let's Clean Up" (CD, tracks, 1, 2) and move to the Singing Circle as you play "Thank the Lord and Sing His Praise" (CD, track 25).

Singing Circle

Provide rhythm instruments for children to play. Encourage them to move and dance to the music.

Sing **First Article Song**

Morning Prayer Song

1 Peter 5:7

All Creatures of Our God and King

Good Morning to You

Happy Birthday to You and **God Made Me His Child** to celebrate special occasions.

I Can Stamp (Add verses to go with each lesson, such as "I can smell things with my nose . . . God gave me this nose.")

Jesus Loves the Little Ones

He's Got the Whole World in His Hands (Variation: "He's Got the Girls and the Boys in His Hands" and "He's Got the Tiny Little Babies in His Hands.")

God Is So Good (Variation: "God Made My Nose . . . He's So Good to Me.")

2 God Speaks
10 minutes

Come to the Worship Center

Have children sit on a special rug or quilt to get ready to hear today's Bible story. Sing or hum "Thank the Lord and Sing His Praise" as everyone gathers. Have a vase to put Sprout's flowers on the altar. Thank everyone for coming so nicely and for being ready to listen. Do the action rhyme "Open Them, Close Them."

Say **In the name of the Father and of the Son and of the Holy Spirit. Amen.** Make the sign of the cross as you say this and invite the children to repeat these holy words with you.

Introducing God's Word

Sprout comes out singing "God Made My Nose, He's So Good to Me" and carrying a bouquet of flowers.

Teacher: Hi, Sprout! What beautiful flowers you brought! May I smell them?

Sprout: Hi, everyone! Yes, you may smell my flowers. The children may smell them too. Don't they smell good?

Teacher: Yes! Thank you for bringing the flowers, Sprout. What are you going to do with them?

Sprout: I want to put some flowers on God's altar. And I'm going to give a flower to each of the boys and girls today. They can take a flower home when it's time to leave.

Teacher: How thoughtful of you, Sprout! The flowers will help us remember that God made our noses, and He makes beautiful things for us to smell in His world.

Sprout: I have a nose too! I love to smell flowers! Thank You, God, for MY nose!

Teacher: Let's put your flowers into a glass of water, Sprout, so they stay fresh. You can give them to the girls and boys before they go home today.

Sprout: That's great! I'll see you later then! Bye!

Telling God's Word

Say **How nice of Sprout to bring flowers today for us to smell. Seeing the flowers reminds me of all the beautiful flowers and bushes that God made in the garden for Adam and Eve to enjoy. Did you see the beautiful flowers on the altar in church?**

Show the God Made Adam and Eve Poster. **Let's find the flowers in the poster. Adam and Eve liked to smell the flowers. God made red flowers, pink flowers, and yellow flowers. All the flowers smelled so good! The bushes and trees, grass and fruit smelled good in the garden where they lived too. God gave them many good smells in the world He made!**

God gives us our noses to smell so many of the things He has made in our world. God is so good! Hold up a few items from the Discovery Center. Ask children to smell them. **Do you like this pinecone smell? God gave us noses to smell things in nature and food too.** Cut an orange during this time rather than having it precut. The scent will be much stronger. **Do you like the smell of this orange? I'll cut it for our snack and you can smell it again as you eat the sections.**

7, 21

Let's sing about our nose and how we can smell. Sing "I Can Stamp" (CD, track 7). Sing the lyrics for today: "I can smell things with my nose . . . God gave me this nose."

Have each child look into the big mirror. **Who do you see? That's [William]! Point to your nose. God made your nose! God cares for you so much!**

Point to the poster of Jesus. **Let's say our Bible Words together. God cares for you!** Say the words and clap the rhythm two or three times. Then sing "1 Peter 5:7" (CD, track 21).

Let's fold our hands and thank God for making our noses to smell.

Have children repeat the words of the prayer after you. Pause at * and repeat the words with them. Encourage parents to use this model to pray with their children at home too.

Pray **Thank You, God, for making my nose.***
Thank You for helping us to smell.*
Thank You for Jesus, our Savior and Friend.*
We know You love us.*
We love You too.*
Amen.*

Snack Time

15

Provide wet wipes for parents to clean the children's hands. Sing the echo prayer "Thank You, God, for This Food" (CD, track 15) as children fold their hands. Provide water or juice to drink. Ask a child to give a napkin and paper plate to each person. Parents will need to help their children serve as helpers.

Say **What a gift! God made our noses to smell. We're happy we can smell the orange slices today. Do you like the almond (or vanilla) smell in the cookies?**

Are you able to smell your water? Do you like the smell of your juice drink?

Liturgy Link

Listen to "Thank the Lord and Sing His Praise" on the CD. Sing along a few times. Remind parents and children to listen for this congregational response during worship. Encourage them to play their Family CD at home and in the car, and to sing along with the music and words as a way of praising God for the world and family members He has made for you!

3 We Live
10 minutes

Growing through God's Word—Parent Talk

A Two-Year-Old Develops Socially

Ask **In what ways have you noticed your child developing socially?** Allow parents to share their observations.

Read Psalm 100:3.

Say **It is God who made us. He made each of us a social creature. He didn't make us so that we would live alone, isolated, without social contacts. God intends for us to develop relationships with Him and with others as we develop and grow.**

Sadly, because sin is part of our human lives, we are often separated from each other and from God. Ask parents if they've felt sad, alone, or disappointed this past week. Sin causes great grief in our lives. **However, in His great love for His creation, He kept His promise to send a Savior.** Read John 3:16. **What do we need? What does God provide through Jesus? How does faith and trust in Jesus make a difference in our lives? How can we remind our children each day of His gift of Jesus in our lives?** Again, discuss concrete ways we can tell and show children the love and forgiveness that He gives us through His grace and mercy first given to us on His cross. Emphasize coming to church and pointing out the visible symbols of God's love that you see there—the font, the cross, the Bible, the altar, pastor, and so on.

Your very young child is a social creature. As he or she starts to identify himself or herself as a separate being from mom and dad, he or she becomes more and more aware of others. Encourage your children to shake Pastor's hand at the end of service—let them know that the pastor shares God's love with them.

Two-year-olds want to be with other children. They want to play side by side, though they usually don't interact at this age. They are beginning to learn to share. "Parallel play" is an important stage in the social development of children as they move from pre-social to social behavior. Children move back and forth between these stages, and it's typical for them to have good social interaction at one time and then revert to pre-social behavior another.

Talk about times when children may go backwards in their social behavior. A move, a new baby's birth, a death, or a negative incidence when playing with someone can cause a child to regress temporarily. **As two-year-olds progress toward more social interaction, they begin developing friendships. You'll notice they begin to greet each other as they come into class and say good-bye or hug when it's time to leave. This is a good time for families with young children to get together socially to encourage and promote Christian friendships.** Encourage parents to form a small care group of "Families with Very Young Children" to gather socially outside of class time.

One of the hardest things for two-year-olds to learn is to share. Young children are possessive of their belongings, seeing them as an extension of themselves. Adults can respect the child's need for a security blanket or special doll or animal and allow a child to bring a special object to church or class. Talk about ways to help children learn to share. When friends come, provide two or more of the same toy; put favorite belongings away for the duration; play my turn/your turn games with the children; verbalize: "After you play with the car, please give it to Peter when the timer rings." Thank children for sharing. Reinforce positive behavior. Emphasize forgiving one another as Jesus forgives us.

We are naturally sinful. As we grow in our awareness of God's love for us and for all people, we reach out in love to others. Our loving Father, through the actions of His Son, Jesus, provided free and complete forgiveness for all our sins. When Jesus died on the cross, He took away all our sins! As we recognize our children's uniqueness, we can encourage them to reach out to others in loving ways. We can remind our children of Jesus' forgiveness when we fail.

11

Move to your Singing Circle area. Sing "God Is So Good" (CD, track 11) while everyone comes together.

4 Closing
10 minutes

Songs and Prayers

Say Show the Toddler Bible you use during storytelling. **Today we heard how God made our noses for us to smell. Let's do this action rhyme together:**

God made you, *(Point to each child.)*
God made me! *(Point to yourself.)*
God loves you, *(Point to each child.)*
God loves me! *(Point to yourself.)*
God made your nose to smell! *(Point to children's noses.)*
God made my nose to smell! *(Point to your nose.)*
God loves you, *(Point to each child.)*
God loves me! *(Point to yourself.)*

Ask **Who has made our noses? That's right, God made our noses! He made the whole world! God gives us so many smells in His world. God cares for us! Let's fold our hands and thank God for**

making our noses to smell so well. You can say the prayer words after I say them.

Pray **Dear God,***
Thank You for making my nose.*
Thank You for helping me smell.*
Thank You that I can smell the flowers and candles in your Church.*
Thank You for Jesus, our Savior and Friend.*
You love us so much!*
We love You too!*
Amen.*

20

Sing "Now It's Time to Say Good-bye" (CD, track 20)

Say Good-bye

Have your Sprout puppet help you say a personal good-bye to each child and his or her parent(s) as you hand a flower to each child.

Say **Take this flower home today. Remember that God has made your nose and He helps you to smell!**

Take Homes

Family Page 4—Encourage parents to review today's Bible lesson, sing, and pray with their children.

Craft Page 4

Lesson 5

God Made the World— God Made My Mouth

Genesis 2

Key Point

God is so good. God made my mouth to taste many good things in His world.

Connections

Bible Words
[God] cares for you. 1 Peter 5:7

Faith Words
God, Jesus, maker

Catechism
Apostles' Creed: First Article
I believe in God the Father Almighty, Maker of heaven and earth.

Liturgy
Thank the Lord and sing His praise; tell everyone what He has done.

Materials Needed

Step		Materials
1 Opening	Teacher Tools	Nametags Teacher CD Craft Page 5: God Made My Mouth
	Other Supplies	See "To Prepare" instructions for each Activity Center
2 God Speaks	Teacher Tools	Teacher CD Sprout Puppet God Made My Mouth to Speak, Sing, and Taste Poster God Made Adam and Eve Poster
	Other Supplies	Poster of Jesus Banana for Sprout Toddler Bible Large mirror
3 We Live	Teacher Tools	Bible
4 Closing	Teacher Tools	Family Page 5
	Other Supplies	Toddler Bible

1 Opening
30 minutes

Welcome

After welcoming each family, direct them to the day's focus: "God Made My Mouth to Taste."

Say **Choose an activity to begin with your child as you focus on God's gift of our mouths and the ability to taste the good things He makes for us in His world.**

Activity Centers

Water

To Prepare: water pan; scoops or pitcher with cups.

Allow children to experience water play or invite them to have a drink and taste the water. Consider having different flavored waters for the children to taste too.

Say **Can you taste the water? What does it taste like? Water is so good for us. God gives us water to drink!**

Art

To Prepare: Craft Page 5: God Made My Mouth; paper plates; precut pictures of food; clothesline or length of cord; clothespins that pinch.

Give each family a "God Made My Mouth" page and crayons.

Say **Color the things God gives us to taste with our mouths. Thank You, God, for the gift of our mouths and our ability to taste!** Color and talk about the pictures. Add stickers to the paper. Remind parents to write the child's name on the back of his or her paper.

Have families glue precut pictures of food items on paper plates as they talk about all the various foods God gives us to eat and taste with our mouths.

Say **God is good! He made our mouths to taste all this good food He makes in our world. What foods do you like? What is your favorite food?**

Some children may attach many food pictures, while others may glue one or two pictures and be finished quickly. Affirm each child's project. Ask parents to write their children's names on the back of the plates. Help children use a pinch-type clothespin to display the food projects on a clothesline.

Play Dough

To Prepare: Play dough; craft sticks; plastic knives.

Say **Let's make pretend food today. What's your favorite food? Can you make an apple? Can you make a slice of pizza? A sandwich? What other foods can you make?**

God gives us many kinds of food to eat. He is so good to us. God cares for us.

Pretend

To Prepare: Bowls; spoons; spatulas; cookie sheets; pots and pans; plastic food; empty food boxes; child's grocery cart.

Have families pretend to grocery shop, "cook," set the table, and feed the baby as they pretend.

Ask **What are you cooking? It smells good. What does it taste like? What do you like to eat? What is your baby eating? Does he like it? God is so good to us. He made our mouths so we can taste and eat our food.**

Say **Let's cook breakfast. What will we make? Does your cereal taste sweet or sour? Does your toast taste hot or cold? Thank You, God, for everything You made in the whole world!**

Books and Puzzles

Simple shape and color puzzles; peg puzzles of people of all ages

Picture and board books about God's creation

Apostles' Creed—Follow and Do by Joni Walker, CPH (56-2336)

Why I Love You, God by Michelle Medlock Adams, CPH (56-2165)

Transition

Sing "Let's Clean Up" (CD, tracks 1, 2) and move to the Singing Circle. As families make the transition, play and sing "Thank the Lord and Sing His Praise" (CD, track 25).

Singing Circle

Provide rhythm instruments for children to play. Encourage them to move and dance to the music.

Sing

First Article Song

Morning Prayer Song

1 Peter 5:7

All Creatures of Our God and King

Good Morning to You

Happy Birthday to You and **God Made Me His Child** to celebrate special occasions.

I Can Stamp (Add verses to go with each lesson, such as "I can taste things with my mouth . . . God gave me this mouth.")

Jesus Loves the Little Ones

He's Got the Whole World in His Hands (Variation: "He's Got the Girls and the Boys in His Hands" and "He's Got the Tiny Little Babies in His Hands.")

God Is So Good (Variation: "God Made My Mouth . . . He's So Good to Me.")

2 God Speaks
10 minutes

Come to the Worship Center

11, 13

Have children sit on a special rug or quilt to get ready to hear today's Bible story. Sing or hum "God is So Good" (CD, track 11) as everyone gathers. Thank everyone for being ready to listen. Do the action rhyme "Open Them, Close Them" (CD, track 13).

Say **In the name of the Father and of the Son and of the Holy Spirit. Amen.** Make the sign of the cross as you say this and invite the children to repeat these holy words with you.

Introducing God's Word

Sprout comes out singing "God Made My Mouth . . . He's So Good to Me" and carrying a banana.

Teacher: Hi, Sprout! We're glad to see you today. You seem very happy.

Sprout: Hi, everyone! It's a great day! I slept so well in my bed. And my breakfast tasted sooooo good!

Teacher: What did you have to eat?

Sprout: My daddy made pancakes on the griddle. He helped me pour strawberry syrup all over them. And then we sliced a banana on top. But that's not all!

Teacher: What else did you have?

Sprout: Mommy helped me squirt whipped cream on top! Yummy!

Teacher: That sounds like a delicious-tasting breakfast, Sprout!

Sprout: Oh, yes, it was! I wish you could have tasted it too! I brought you a banana to share with the girls and boys today.

Teacher: Thank you, Sprout! We'll taste the banana during our Snack Time. It was nice of you to think of us.

Sprout: God made such a great world! And God made many good foods for us to eat.

Teacher: That's right. Let's look at some of those foods together.

Telling God's Word

Show the God Made My Mouth to Speak, Sing, and Taste Poster.

Say **God gives us our mouths to speak and sing and to taste so many things He has made in our world. God is so good!** Point to each item on the poster. **What is this? Do you like to taste food? Thank you God for all the good food you give us that we can taste. What does this food taste like? Do you like to sing with your mouth? Do you pray with your mouth? Thank you, God, for my mouth that can sing and pray to you!**

Show the poster "God Made Adam and Eve." **When God made the**

first people, Adam and Eve, He made them a beautiful garden where they lived. God made many beautiful trees and bushes to grow in the garden. He gave Adam and Eve each a mouth so they could eat fruit and berries from the trees and bushes. He gave them grapes to eat and He gave them raspberries to eat. What other foods do you think God made for Adam and Eve to eat? God also gave Adam and Eve mouths to speak to each other and to God.

God cares for us. He is so good to make our mouths and give us so many good things to taste. Jesus gives us His body and blood to eat and drink in church. Does Pastor give your mommies and daddies a special drink and bread to eat in church? One day, you will taste this special meal, The Lord's Supper! Point to the picture of the parents taking Holy Communion.

7, 21

Let's sing about our mouth and how we can taste. Sing "I Can Stamp" (CD, track 7). Sing the lyrics for today: "I can taste things with my mouth . . . God gave me this mouth."

Have each child look into the big mirror. **Who do you see? Look, I see [Kari]! Point to your mouth. God made your mouth! God cares for you so much!**

Point to the poster of Jesus. **Let's say our Bible Words together. God cares for you!** Say the words and clap the rhythm two or three times. Then sing "1 Peter 5:7" (CD, track 21).

Say **Let's fold our hands and thank God for making our mouths so we can taste our food.**

Have children repeat the words of the prayer after you. Pause at * and repeat the words with them. Encourage parents to use this model to pray with their children at home too.

Pray
Thank You, God, for making my mouth.*
Thank You for helping us to taste and sing and pray*
Thank You for Jesus, our Savior and Friend*
We know You love us.*
We love You too.*
Amen.*

Teacher Tip

By establishing a routine in your class, children will learn to know what to expect, and with time, you will notice that they will begin to participate in saying, singing, clapping, and doing things with you. Always encourage the adults to participate and help their children do the same.

Snack Time

15

Provide wet wipes for parents to clean the children's hands. Sing "Thank You, God, for This Food" (CD, track 15) as children fold their hands. Provide water or juice to drink.

Ask a child to give a napkin and paper plate to each person. Parents will help their children choose various food items to taste today. Slice the banana that Sprout brought to share.

Say **God made the whole world! He made our mouths so that we can taste our food and drink. We thank God for our mouths so we can taste. Do you like the salty taste of the pretzels? The sour taste of the pickle? The sweet taste of the juice?**

Say a short action rhyme and have families echo:

Say
God gave me a mouth *(Point to mouth.)*
So I can eat *(Pretend to put food into mouth and chew.)*

Liturgy Link

Listen to "Thank the Lord and Sing His Praise" on the CD (track 25). Sing along a few times. Remind parents and children to listen for this congregational response during worship.

Bread and cheese *(Pretend to eat.)*
And bananas so sweet. *(Pretend to eat.)*

3 We Live
10 minutes

Growing through God's Word—Parent Talk

A Two-Year-Old Develops Intellectually

Ask **In what ways have you noticed your child developing intellectually?** Allow parents to share their observations. **Children use all their senses to grow in the knowledge of the world God made, which includes them!**

Read 2 Peter 3:18.

Say **As young children see, hear, smell, touch, and taste, they learn informally. Sensory experiences are necessary for each of us to learn and grow in our understanding of God's world around us. We need to provide many informal experiences and hands-on activities for young children's memory banks to develop.**

Young children need much repetition as they learn. What activities does your child like to do? Have parents share, reinforcing the need for children to play as they develop their senses. **As children hear stories, see illustrations, taste foods, visit places, smell odors, and touch toys and objects, they begin to make connections, build background information, and develop language, math, and reading skills.**

Young children need concrete learning experiences. What are ways we can provide concrete learning activities in our everyday living? Let your child help stir the cookie dough. Let him help sweep the garage with you. Let her help feed the dog or cat. Have your child DO activities with you. Children remember what they actively DO.

Your child learns and grows intellectually through play. She learns to cooperate, think logically, take turns, formulate ideas and move from concrete to abstract thinking as she grows older. Play helps lengthen a child's attention span. Play helps develop math, science, reading, and language skills.

Pretend with your child. Line up chairs to become a train. Cover a table with a blanket to create a cave. Wear costumes and dress-up clothes for playacting. Play children's musical instruments together in a band.

Play enhances skills in many areas and stimulates intellectual development. Provide lots of unstructured time for your child to play.

When children and adults play and work, we do so as sinful humans. We can't live a perfect life because of the sin we are

born with. Thankfully, God kept His promise to send a Savior to the sinful world. So, most importantly, remind your child of Jesus' love and forgiveness for him or her and for you. Taste and see that the Lord is good (Psalm 34:8)**! Go often to the altar to eat and drink the body and blood of your Savior. Receive with your mouth this heavenly gift and with it, forgiveness, life, and salvation! Take your child with you to the altar. Talk about God's special meal, speak highly of it and how important it is to you. This will help your child develop a positive view of this Sacrament and its benefits—both now and for eternity.**

Because God first loved us, we can love others. Jesus showed His love by doing what His Father sent Him to earth to do—to die on the cross so that we could be forgiven, to come alive again so that through His promise we can also live forever someday in heaven. What a gift—the best gift God could ever give us!

25

Read aloud about this gift—Ephesians 2:8–9.

Move to your Singing Circle area. Sing "Thank the Lord and Sing His Praise" (CD, track 25) while everyone comes together.

4 Closing

10 minutes

Songs and Prayers

Say Show the Toddler Bible you use during storytelling. **Today, we heard how God made our mouths for us to taste. Let's do this action rhyme together:**

God made you, *(Point to each child.)*
God made me! *(Point to yourself.)*
God loves you, *(Point to each child.)*
God loves me! *(Point to yourself.)*
God made your mouth to taste! *(Point to children's mouths.)*
God made my mouth to taste! *(Point to your mouth.)*
God made your mouth to sing! *(Point to each child.)*
God made my mouth to sing! *(Point to your mouth.)*
God made your mouth to pray! *(Point to each child.)*
God made my mouth to pray! *(Point to your mouth.)*
God loves you, *(Point to each child.)*
God loves me! *(Point to yourself.)*

Ask **Who has made your mouth? That's right, God made your mouth! God cares for us! Let's fold our hands and thank God for making our mouths to taste so well. You can say the prayer words after I say them.**

Pray **Dear God,***
Thank You for making my mouth.*
Thank You for helping me taste and sing and pray*
Thank You for Jesus, my Savior and Friend.*
You love us so much!*
We love You too!*
Amen.*

Sing "Now It's Time to Say Good-bye" (CD, track 20)

Say Good-bye

Say **When you eat lunch today, remember that God made your mouth and helps you to taste!**

Take Homes

Family Page 5—Encourage parents to review today's Bible lesson, sing, and pray with their children.

Craft Page 5

Lesson 6

God Made the World—God Made My Hands

Genesis 2

Key Point

God is so good. God made my hands to do and feel things in His wonderful world.

Connections

Bible Words
[God] cares for you. 1 Peter 5:7

Faith Words
God, Jesus, maker

Catechism
Apostles' Creed: First Article
I believe in God the Father Almighty, Maker of heaven and earth.

Liturgy
Thank the Lord and sing His praise; tell everyone what He has done.

Hymn
All Creatures of Our God and King (*Lutheran Worship* 436)

Materials Needed

1 Opening

Teacher Tools
- Nametags
- Teacher CD
- Craft Page 6: God Made My Hands

Other Supplies
- See "To Prepare" instructions for each Activity Center

2 God Speaks

Teacher Tools
- Teacher CD
- Sprout puppet
- God Made My Hands to Touch Poster
- God Made Adam and Eve Poster

Other Supplies
- Storytelling objects in a bag
- Poster of Jesus
- Toddler Bible
- Large mirror
- Bible Story Booklet

3 We Live

Teacher Tools
- Bible

4 Closing

Teacher Tools
- Family Page 6

Other Supplies
- Toddler Bible

1 Opening
30 minutes

Welcome

Greet families by name as they enter the room. Ask them to focus on "God Made My Hands" as they choose activities to begin.

Say **God has made our hands as a gift for us to touch, feel, and do.**

Activity Centers

Water

To Prepare: Water pan; scoops; pitcher of water; large bowl; paper towels.

Provide the water pan and scoops for children to experience water play, using their hands to feel the water and the tools. Or provide liquid soap, water in a pitcher, a large bowl, and paper towels. (Or forego this center for today.)

Ask **God made your hands and God made the water. Can you wash your hands with the water and the soap?** Put soap in their palm and pour water over their hands into the bowl as they wash them. **God washed your sins away with water and His Word when you were baptized. The pastor used his hands to pour water over you and said, "I baptize you in the name of the Father and of the Son and of the Holy Spirit."**

Rice

To Prepare: Dry rice; dish pan; scoops; funnels; plastic cups.

Put about 3 inches of dry rice in a plastic dishpan or storage container. Add scoops, funnels, and plastic cups. Encourage children to scoop the rice from cup to cup, feeling the textures of the materials.

Ask **What does the rice feel like? Is it bumpy? Smooth? Wet? Dry? God gives us hands so we can feel the rice and the cups. God helps us use our hands to do things and to feel things.**

Art

To Prepare: Craft Page 6: God Made My Hands; stickers.

As families color and talk about the "God Made My Hands" page, they can add stickers as they say, **Thank You, God, for the gift of our hands.**

Have parents use a pencil to draw around the child's hands on paper, then outline the hands with a brightly colored marker. Let children scribble-color their hands,.

Say **God has made your hands wonderful. Look at your fingers? Can you wiggle them? Can you clap your hands? God gave you hands to help you do so many things—play with toys, eat your food, help put your clothes on, hold a book, open doors, and even share toys with friends.**

Play Dough

To Prepare: Play dough; craft sticks; plastic knives; rolling pins; round plastic bottles.

Say **We can do so many things with our hands! Can you roll the play dough? Make a handprint in your play dough pie. Pinch the play dough like this. Use the knife or craft stick to cut play dough strips. We thank God for our hands!**

Discovery

To Prepare: Various items used in worship.

Ask an elder or altar guild member to bring one of your pastor's stoles, a neck cross, and a chalice, and assist the children in touching these things. Or invite your pastor come and do this with the children. Let the kids hold a hymnal and turn the pages in it. Give them a church bulletin. Tell them that these things all help us worship and learn about Jesus.

Say **Can you use your hands to touch these special things? Where do you see these things? Who holds them with their hand?**

Pretend

To Prepare: Items in a "housekeeping center"—doll babies, blankets, stroller, plastic food, dishes, play clothes.

Have families dress a baby doll, take a walk with the stroller, cook a meal, put the baby to bed, and other everyday life activities. As they do these things, interact with the children to help them learn about their sense of touch and the gift of hands God gives them.

Ask **How does the baby's blanket feel? Can you find something that feels hard? What does the plastic stroller feel like? Rough? Smooth? We are glad God gave us hands to feel things and to help do things.**

Books and Puzzles

Simple shape and color puzzles; peg puzzles of people of all ages

Picture and board books about God's creation

Apostles' Creed—Follow and Do by Joni Walker, CPH (56-2336)

Why I Love You, God by Michelle Medlock Adams, CPH (56-2165)

Transition

Sing "Let's Clean Up" (CD, tracks 1, 2) and move to the Singing Circle. Play "Thank the Lord and Sing His Praise" (CD, track 25). Sing along with the music as you make the transition.

Singing Circle

Provide rhythm instruments for children to play. Encourage them to move and dance to the music.

Sing **First Article Song**

Morning Prayer Song

1 Peter 5:7

All Creatures of Our God and King

Good Morning to You

Happy Birthday to You and **God Made Me His Child** to celebrate special occasions.

Teacher Tip

Scribble-coloring is all that is expected of two-year-olds; by using chunky crayons, they enjoy the activity and learn eye-to-hand control while coloring. Parents should write their children's names on the backs of their papers.

I Can Stamp ("I can clap and wave and pound. God gave me these hands.")

Jesus Loves the Little Ones

He's Got the Whole World in His Hands (Variation: "He's Got the Girls and the Boys in His Hands" and "He's Got the Tiny Little Babies in His Hands.")

God Is So Good (Variation: "God Made My Hands. He's So Good to Me.")

2 God Speaks
10 minutes

Come to the Worship Center

Have children sit on a special rug to get ready to hear today's Bible story. Sing "God Is So Good" as everyone gathers. Thank everyone for being ready to listen.

Say **In the name of the Father and of the Son and of the Holy Spirit. Amen.** Make the sign of the cross as you say this and invite the children to repeat these holy words with you.

Introducing God's Word

Sprout comes out singing "God Made My Hands . . . He's So Good to Me" and carrying a bag of objects having a variety of textures for children to feel. Have at least one object per child in your class.

Teacher: Hi, Sprout! We're glad to see you today. What did you bring with you?

Sprout: Hi, everyone! This is my surprise bag. I brought it so we can play a game with the girls and boys and their families.

Teacher: That sounds like fun, Sprout. What do we do?

Sprout: Well, each child picks one thing out of my surprise bag. We'll see what it is, tell what it feels like, and tell what we do with it.

Teacher: Okay! Everyone will get a turn. Let's start with [choose a child]. Parents, you may help your children.

Say **God cares for you, [Andrew], and He gave you hands to feel. What is this? How does it feel? What do we do with it? We're so glad God gave you the gift of hands to feel and do things in His world!**

Continue by having each child choose an object, feel it, and then tell what we can do with it. Families will need to help their children with this activity. Many two-year-olds may not be talking yet. So help them verbalize when necessary. Still, they are soaking up what you say and do. We can trust that through God's Word, the Spirit is working in their hearts and minds!

Sprout: Boys and girls, you did a GREAT job! Thanks for playing my game with me. Now I need my surprise things back in my bag. Thank you!

Teacher: We had fun playing your game, Sprout. We'll see you next time. Bye!

Say **Boys and girls, I'm glad God gave us hands. They are a beautiful gift with which we can touch and do things.**

Telling God's Word

Say Hold the Toddler Bible open. **God tells us in the Bible, His Word, that He has made everything good. He loves us and cares for us.**

Let's remember all the things He has made for us. Review the concept of God being our maker—show each page of the Child's Bible Storybook so far.

God made the world and He said it was good. The world is God's gift to us!

God made you and me—He made our bodies so wonderfully. Our bodies are gifts to us.

God made our eyes to see.

God made our ears to hear.

God made our noses to smell.

God made our mouths to taste.

God made our hands to feel and touch.

All these are very special gifts. God helps us use all the parts of our bodies to enjoy His world. God cares for you and me so much!

Show the God Made My Hands to Touch Poster. **When you hold your daddy's hand, what does it feel like? How do your hands move? What do your hands feel when you hug someone special? What is hot? What feels prickly? The thorns are sharp, aren't they? Talk about how each item feels. What does money feel like?**

Show the God Made Adam and Eve Poster. **God made the first people, Adam and Eve, and gave them hands to feel the beautiful things in God's garden. They used their hands to take care of the trees, flowers, and animals.**

6, 21

Let's sing about our hands and how God helps us to use them. Sing "I Can Stamp" (CD, track 6). Sing the lyrics for today: "I can clap and wave and pound . . . God gave me these hands." (Do the motions.)

Have each child look into the big mirror. **Who do you see? Look, I see [Benjamin]! Wave your hands. Clap your hands. Thank You, God, for the gift of Benjamin's hands!**

Point to the poster of Jesus. **Let's say our Bible Words together. God cares for you!** Say the words and clap the rhythm two or three times. Sing "1 Peter 5:7" (CD, track 21) at this time.

Let's fold our hands to pray and thank God for making our hands to touch and feel.

Have children repeat the words of the prayer after you. Pause at * and repeat the words with them. Encourage parents to use this model to pray at home too.

Liturgy Link

Listen to "Thank the Lord and Sing His Praise" on the CD (track 25). Sing along a few times as everyone moves to the table for snacks.

Pray **Thank You, God, for making my hands.*
Thank You for helping me feel and do things.*
Thank You, God, for Jesus, my Savior and Friend.*
We know You love us.*
We love You too.*
Amen.***

Snack Time

Provide wet wipes for parents to clean their children's hands.

Say **Let's fold our hands that God made for us and sing our snack prayer.**

Sing "Thank You, God, for This Food" echo prayer (CD, track 15). Provide water or juice to drink.

15

Say **Now we'll use our hands to be helpers.** Ask a child to give a napkin and paper plate to each person. Parents will help their children.

God made our hands to help us feel things. How do the pretzels feel? Smooth or bumpy? How does the Jell-O feel? Rough or smooth? Our hands are God's gifts to us. Thank You, God!

3 We Live
10 minutes

Growing through God's Word—Parent Talk

Ministering to the Whole Child

Read 1 John 4:19.

Say **Today, we're talking about what your child needs as a** whole child. **God created each of us as whole persons with physical, emotional, spiritual, social, and intellectual needs. Though we can talk about each area separately, we can't divide our children into separate pieces. They learn about the world as** whole children **and by total involvement in everything they do.**

The biggest need that children and adults have is that of a Savior. We're each born sinful. In our sin, we are enemies of God and want nothing to do with Him. We are rebellious children who want to go our own way. God in His love sought us and found us through water and His Word, giving us His Son, Jesus, to die on the cross to take our sins away and restore us to Him. He loves us that much! Jesus rose from the dead and now He gives us forgiveness, life, and the certain hope of living forever with Him when we die. Our children need His love and forgiveness too. Our love and forgiveness toward them reflects God's love and forgiveness. "We love because He first loved us."

Share ideas about how we can make the Gospel—Good News—real for very young children every day, from morning until bedtime! **What**

would you say and do when your child wakes up grumpy? When he throws his breakfast on the floor? When your friend or spouse says something hurtful to you? Help parents apply the Gospel to life situations!

Can you think of experiences that involve the whole child **as he or she learns?** Allow parents to share ideas. Then suggest, if they don't, nature walks, trips to the zoo or museums, and adding hands-on experiences to their children's everyday living, such as helping to make a bed, clean the table, brush the dog, and put away toys in "category" bins.

Go on a 'field trip' to the church sanctuary and go up to the altar and the font, let your child touch them, hold them up in the pulpit to see what the pastor sees. If the organist is there, ask them if your child can play a note or listen as the organist plays a note.

Children learn differently than adults learn. Learning to walk isn't just a physical skill. It involves intellectual, social, and emotional learning. Teaching the whole child **involves his or her participation in learning activities—a hands-on approach—as the child connects the activity with the muscular movement, socialization, and spiritual aspects of life. As she or he helps put lunch out, she or he learns the physical movement of food preparation, the social interaction with mommy or daddy, the emotional aspect of being a good helper (the high esteem in doing something well), the recognition of God's goodness in giving us the food we need, and the intellect needed to prepare food with utensils or pans.**

Give your child appropriate stimulation, direction, and encouragement to grow in ALL areas of development. What is the danger of over-emphasizing, for example, intellectual development while neglecting other areas? Allow parents to share thoughts.

Remember that everyone is different. Because of sin in our world, not everyone enjoys the gift of perfect sight and hearing, walking, communicating or learning easily. We acknowledge and accept differences while we praise God for all the gifts He gives. We put special needs and requests into His hands through prayer, by supporting parents and children, and through our acceptance of differences. If families have children who require special needs, remind everyone to include them in prayer, and encourage small care groups to meet regularly for parents and children to develop friendships.

Most important, praise and thank God for the gifts of the children's bodies and all the senses He has given them to use in the world He has made for us. God loves and cares for each of us. His greatest gift to us is Jesus. He has made us His children in His family!

Move to your Singing Circle area. Sing "God Is So Good" as all come together.

4 Closing
10 minutes

Songs and Prayers

Say Show the Toddler Bible you use during storytelling. **Today, we heard how God made our hands for us to touch and do things. What a wonderful gift our hands are from God! Let's do this action rhyme together:**

God made you, *(Point to each child.)*
God made me! *(Point to yourself.)*
God made your hands to clap! *(Clap hands.)*
God made my hands to clap! *(Clap hands.)*
God loves you, *(Point to each child.)*
God loves me! *(Point to yourself.)*

Ask **Who has made your hands? That's right, God made your hands! He made the whole world! God cares for us! Our hands are gifts from Him. Let's fold our hands and thank God for our hands. You can say the prayer words after I say them.**

Pray **Dear God,***
Thank You for making my hands.*
Thank You for hands that feel and do things.*
Thank You for Jesus, my Savior and Friend.*
You love us so much!*
We love You too!*
Amen.*

20

Sing "Now It's Time to Say Good-bye" (CD, track 20)

Say Good-bye

Say **As you go home, think of all the ways your hands do things and feel things. Thank God for His gift of hands!**

Take Homes

Family Page 6—Encourage parents to review today's Bible lesson, sing and pray with their children.

Craft Page 6

Lesson 7

God Made the World—God Made Me His Child in Baptism

Romans 6:4

Key Point

God makes us His children through His Word and the water of Baptism.

Connections

Bible Words
I have called you by name, you are Mine. Isaiah 43:1

Faith Words
God, Jesus, Baptism

Catechism
Apostles' Creed: First Article
I believe in God the Father Almighty, Maker of heaven and earth.

Liturgy
Thank the Lord and sing His praise; tell everyone what He has done.

Hymn
All Creatures of Our God and King (*Lutheran Worship* 436)

Materials Needed

1 Opening

Teacher Tools
- Nametags
- Teacher CD
- Craft Page 7: God Made Me His Child in Baptism
- Reproducible Page 1

Other Supplies
- See "To Prepare" instructions for each Activity Center
- Rhythm ribbons or scarves

2 God Speaks

Teacher Tools
- Teacher CD
- Sprout Puppet
- God Makes Me His Child in Baptism Poster

Other Supplies
- Poster of Jesus
- Toddler Bible
- Bowl of water, seashell, Bible

3 We Live

Teacher Tools
- Bible

4 Closing

Teacher Tools
- Family Page 7

Other Supplies
- Child's baptismal banner

1 Opening
30 minutes

Welcome

Welcome children and adults warmly and allow friendship-building time as families become involved in the learning activities.

Focus on thanking God for the world He made and for the new life He gives us through Baptism.

Activity Centers

Water

To Prepare: vinyl tablecloth; plastic wash pan; water; measuring cups; small plastic drinking cups; small washcloths; a water-usable plastic baby doll, shells.

Cover a table with a vinyl tablecloth and place a plastic pan with about 3 inches of water on the tablecloth.

Say **We can wash the baby. God gives us water for bath time. How good it is to be washed and clean! Do you like bath time?**

When the pastor pours water on our head, he says, "I baptize you in the name of the Father and of the Son and of the Holy Spirit." Let's use a shell to scoop and pour water three times. God the Father, God the Son, God the Holy Spirit. Through the water and God's Word He makes us His children!

Art

To Prepare: Craft Page 7: God Made Me His Child in Baptism; cross stickers; large, dark blue paper for background; Reproducible Page 1; green felt, 10 × 12 inches; dowel rod; yarn; felt rain drop shapes; felt shell shape; craft glue; child's name and baptismal date printed on card stock about 1 × 8 inches.

"God Made Me His Child in Baptism" page—As families color and talk about the page, they can add a cross sticker, and use the glue stick to attach the seashell and three paper rain drop shapes from Reproducible Page 1.

Say **God made the world and God made you! When you were baptized, God made you His dear child.**

Or glue the white paper shell shape and the paper raindrop shapes to a large, dark blue background paper. Add the strip of paper showing the child's name and baptismal date. (If a child has not been baptized, simply add his or her name.)

Say **When you were baptized, the pastor put water on your head three times and said, "I baptize you in the name of the Father, Son, and Holy Spirit." God made you His child!**

Fabric baptismal banner: Before class, sew a casing about ½-inch wide across the top of each child's green felt banner pieces. Have parents use craft glue to help children attach the seashell, raindrop shapes, and the child's name paper to the green felt background. Put the dowel rod in the casing along the top of the banner. Add a length of yarn for a hanger.

Play Dough

To Prepare: Set out various colors of play dough and assorted cookie cutters.

Ask **What can you make that is new? A new flower? A new ball? A new cookie shape? God makes you and me new when we are baptized. He makes us His children.**

The pastor might use a seashell or his hand to put the water on our heads three times. Can you make one, two, three water drops with your play dough?

Discovery

To Prepare: Precut pictures of babies, children, and adults; 3 × 5 inch cards; three baskets or plastic containers; baptismal items—candle, certificate, gown, photos.

Repeat this Activity Center from Lesson 1 and add Baptism items and pictures/photos that you and/or the families have brought to look at, talk about and sort today.

Glue one picture of a baby, child, or adult onto each file card. Help children sort the pictures into the three different categories and place them into containers.

Say **Yes, that's a baby. When you were a baby, you couldn't feed yourself. We gave you a bottle and your baby food. Now you can use a spoon. God helps babies grow. God helps you grow.**

Who is this girl or boy? What can boys and girls do? God helps them run and jump, read and pray, sing and dance. Refer to any older siblings and how God cares for them.

Here's a mommy. Here's a daddy. God helps mommies and daddies work and play. He helps us take care of you. Mommies and daddies bring children to church to sing and learn together.

See what the pastor is doing in this picture or photo. He's pouring water on the baby's head to baptize him. When we're baptized, God makes us His dear children. Show a candle, a baptismal gown, a baptismal certificate, and pictures/photos of children's Baptisms.

Pretend

To Prepare: Baby dolls; blankets; baby care items; small rocking chair.

As children take care of the baby dolls,

Say **God gives parents a baby to love. You're taking good care of your baby doll. God loves all the babies and boys and girls. He loves us so much that He makes us His children, and part of His family. When we are baptized, we join God's family!**

Books and Puzzles

Simple shape and color puzzles; peg puzzles

Picture and board books about God's creation

God Makes Me His Child in Baptism by Janet Wittenback, CPH (56-1537)

Holy Baptism—Follow and Do by Joni Walker CPH (56-2334)

Transition

Remind families they have a few minutes to finish their activities before putting items away. Then sing "Let's Clean Up" (CD, tracks 1, 2) and move to face each other in a Singing Circle area.

Singing Circle

Very young children need opportunities to move their bodies and get their wiggles out. Singing Circle time is a wonderful opportunity to sing together, move to the music, wave colorful scarves or ribbons (to suggest flowing water), and do simple actions to the lyrics.

Sing **First Article Song**

Morning Prayer Song

Isaiah 43:1

1 Peter 4:7

All Creatures of Our God and King

Good Morning to You

Happy Birthday or **God Made Me His Child** to celebrate special occasions.

Jesus Loves the Little Ones

He's Got the Whole World in His Hands (Variation: "He's Got the Girls and the Boys in His Hands" and "He's Got the Tiny Little Babies in His Hands.")

God Is So Good (Variation: "God Makes Me His.")

2 God Speaks

10 minutes

Come to the Worship Center

Have children sit on a special rug, blanket, or quilt to get ready to hear today's Bible story. Sing or hum "God Is So Good" (CD, track 11) or "Isaiah 43:1" (CD, track 22) as everyone gathers. Thank everyone for coming so nicely and for being ready to listen. Encourage the children to say the invocation and make the sign of the cross with you.

Say **In the name of the Father and of the Son and of the Holy Spirit. Amen.**

Introducing God's Word

Sprout comes rushing in, out of breath.

Sprout: Guess what I just saw! Oh, hi, everybody! Just guess!

Teacher: I don't know, Sprout. Please tell us what you just saw!

Sprout: I was walking by the church doors with my daddy. I saw a mommy and a daddy and the man wearing the robes.

Teacher: That's Pastor [name].

Sprout: Guess what they did to the baby! They gave the baby a bath right in church! The pastor washed the baby's head one, two, three times! It was amazing!

Teacher: You saw something wonderful happen, Sprout. You saw a baby being baptized!

Sprout: Baptized? What does being baptized mean?

Teacher: God made the baby His own child when the pastor put water on the baby's head one, two, three times in the name of the Father, Son, and Holy Spirit. He washed the baby's sins away with the water and God's Word.

Sprout: The baby's mommy and daddy looked very happy!

Teacher: They are happy, Sprout, because their baby is God's child, part of God's family and his sins are washed away.

Sprout: Wow! Do you know anyone who has been baptized?

Teacher: Yes, I have been baptized, and these children [some of these children] have been baptized too, Sprout.

Sprout: Wow! That's neat! What was it like when you were baptized? Was the water cold? Do you remember what your pastor said? Were people happy that day?

Teacher: Let's let the parents tell about their children's Baptisms, Sprout.

Have parents tell about their children's baptismal days—who was there, what their child wore, what special mementos they received, and show photos if they brought them. Or show and tell about items related to your own children's baptismal days.

Telling God's Word

If possible, take the children into the sanctuary and tell the story as they sit around the baptismal font.

Show the poster "God Makes Me His Child in Baptism" and the poster of Jesus.

Say **Jesus loves babies and all children. He loves you too! God tells us in the Bible, "I have called you by name, you are Mine." God knows your name, [Gina]! God knows your name, [Timothy]! Tell each child that good news! God knows my name too.**

Show the bowl of water, the Bible, and the seashell. **God uses water and His Word to make you and me His dear children. Maybe when you were a baby your parents took you to church and had you baptized. The pastor might have used a seashell or his hand to pour a little water on your head as he said these words** (Say the following, repeating the dipping and pouring of water three times)**: [Ryan], I baptize you in the name of the Father and of the Son and of the Holy Spirit. Just like that, you belonged to God and your sins were washed away! I'm glad to know that I was baptized and I belong to God. Are you glad too?**

Teacher Tip

Be aware by looking at the family information page to see who has been baptized. If children and/or parents in your class are not yet baptized, assure them that God loves them dearly as His children. Offer to tell them more about Baptism after class. Offer to go with them to talk with your pastor about being baptized in the future.

Say **Wow! God loves you and me so much! We are all God's children!**

17

Let's say our Bible Words together. I have called you by name, you are mine. Clap with the rhythm of the words as you repeat the Bible Words two or three times. Then sing along with the CD as you play "Isaiah 43:1" (CD, track 17).

Now let's fold our hands and thank God for making us His children.

Have children repeat the words of the prayer after you. Pause at the * and repeat the words with them.

Pray **Thank You, God, for loving me.***
We love You too.*
Thank You for making me Your child in Baptism.*
Thank You for Jesus, our Savior and Friend.*
Amen.*

Snack Time

15, 5

Provide wet wipes for parents to clean the children's hands. Sing "Thank You, God, for This Food" (CD, track 15) as children fold their hands and learn that we thank God for the food and drink He gives us to enjoy.

Provide water or juice to drink. Have parents give their children a few people-shaped cookies or crackers.

Or serve blue Jell-O jigglers cut in water drop shapes as a reminder of baptismal water.

Or bring individual cupcakes and a birthday candle for each child to pretend to light. Sing "God Made Me His Child" together (CD, track 5).

Say **God has made us each His dear children. We can light a candle to remember our baptismal birthday—the day God made us part of His family.**

Liturgy Link

Listen to "Thank the Lord and Sing His Praise" on the CD (track 25). Sing along a few times. Remind parents and children to listen for this congregational response. Encourage them to tell others what Jesus has done for us!

3 We Live
10 minutes

Growing through God's Word—Parent Talk

What Does Your Baptism Mean to You?

While children eat their snacks and everyone gathers around one large table, lead the parents through the following dialogue and questions. If you have a team leader, he or she may take the children to an area of the room to have a short playtime or to hear additional storybooks related to today's Bible lesson.

Ask **What does your Baptism mean to you?** Allow parents to share.

Say **Just as God created your child's physical body, God the Holy Spirit also creates a saving faith in each child through water and His Word in Holy Baptism. When you bring your child to be baptized, you fulfill the first responsibility God gives you in your vocation as a parent to help your child develop spiritually.**

God made you His child through Baptism. He makes your child His own dear child in the same way.

Read Psalm 51:5.

Say **Each of us is born sinful. We can't do anything to save ourselves. Sin separates us from God and His love.** Talk about specific ways we fail each day in our relationships with others and with God. **Sin affects all our lives, in the things we do, think, or say that are sinful or the things that we neglect to do, think, and say. We also suffer the affects of sin in the world—sickness, hardship, and evil. The weight of sin is very great, so great that it cost our Savior His life! It's easy to be crushed by sin or our own guilt. But God in His goodness knows what we need! And we know that God kept His promise to save us.**

Read John 3:16.

Say **God didn't leave us in our sin. Through the Living Word, His Son, Jesus, God gives us forgiveness and life and salvation!—free gifts.**

In the Sacrament of Holy Baptism, God, through water and His Word, makes us His dear children, members of His family, with Jesus as our Brother. God creates faith in our hearts at Baptism so that we become heirs of His kingdom. When we die, we will live in heaven with Him. We are washed clean, our sins are no more. Read more in Galatians 3:26–27 and 1 Peter 3:21 about the saving power of Baptism.

Martin Luther encourages us to make the sign of the cross and remember our Baptism each day. Do you know how to make the sign of the cross? We have been doing it at the start of each lesson. Have you attempted to teach your child how to make this visible sign of faith? This is the sign that was made over you and your child at Baptism. Here's how to make the sign of the cross: Simply put your thumb together with your two top fingers and touch your forehead, move down to your chest, and then touch one shoulder and then the next. Children are eager to learn hand motions. This simple gesture can become for you and your child a very visible confession of faith, made at the start and end of each day as you remember that it was upon the cross that Jesus made it possible for you to become God's child. A simple prayer, "Thank You, God, for making me Your child" helps to begin our day.

As your child sees and hears you thanking God for a new day of life as His child, forgiving and loving each other, his or her faith is nourished also. What evidence of saving faith do you see in your child? Take time to share. Encourage one another to live as God's dear children.

22

Move from the table back to your Singing Circle area. Play "Isaiah 43:1" (CD, track 22) and sing along as everyone comes together.

4 Closing
10 minutes

Songs and Prayers

Ask **What did we learn today? Yes, we heard how God cares for each of us so much. We heard how He makes us His children in Baptism.** Have parents and children do the following action rhyme with you.

Say **Splashing water,** *(Wiggle your fingers.)*
God's own Word, *(Make a Bible-book with your hands.)*
We are children of the Lord! *(Raise your arms high and wave them.)*
Splashing water, *(Wiggle your fingers.)*
One, two, three! *(Count to three with your fingers.)*
God made us in His family! *(Raise your arms high and wave them.)*

Ask **Who makes us His dear children? That's right! God does, because He loves us so much! Let's thank God for making us His children. Let's fold our hands. You can say the prayer words after I say the words.**

Pray **Dear God,***
Thank You for making us*
Your children in Baptism.*
Thank you for Jesus, our Savior and Friend.*
We love You!*
Amen.*

20

Sing "Now It's Time to Say Good-bye" (CD, track 20)

Say Good-bye

Say **Good-bye, child of God. Remember how much God loves you when you wash your face, brush your teeth, take a bath, and use water in so many ways. Celebrate your Baptism and say, "Thank You, God, for making me Your child."**

Take Homes

Family Page 7—Encourage parents to glean ideas to use throughout the week as they review, sing, and pray with their children.

Craft Page 7

Lesson 8

God Made the World—God Made Water

Genesis 1:9–10

Key Point

We celebrate God and the water He makes for us. God baptizes us through water and His Word to make us His dear children in His family.

Connections

Bible Words
God saw that it was good. Genesis 1:10

Faith Words
God, Jesus, maker

Catechism
Apostles' Creed: First Article
I believe in God the Father Almighty, Maker of heaven and earth.

Liturgy
Thank the Lord and sing His praise; tell everyone what He has done.

Hymn
All Creatures of Our God and King (*Lutheran Worship* 436)

Materials Needed

1 Opening

Teacher Tools
- Nametags
- Teacher CD
- Craft Page 8: God Made Water

Other Supplies
- See "To Prepare" instructions for each Activity Center
- Rhythm ribbons or scarves

2 God Speaks

Teacher Tools
- Sprout Puppet
- God Made the Water Poster

Other Supplies
- Poster of Jesus
- Cup for puppet
- Toddler Bible
- *This Is the World God Made* (CPH)
- Bowl of water, seashell

3 We Live

Teacher Tools
- Bible

4 Closing

Teacher Tools
- Family Page 8

1 Opening
30 minutes

Welcome

Greet adults and children by name as they come into class. Encourage parents to spend time with their children at one or more of the Activity Centers, focusing on thanking God for the rain and water He gives us.

Activity Centers

Water

To Prepare: pans; cups; funnel; sponge; play food; baby doll.

Cover a table with a vinyl tablecloth and place a plastic pan with about 3 inches of water on the tablecloth. Have children pour water from one cup to another. Provide measuring cups, small plastic drinking cups, a small funnel, a small sponge, a few plastic pieces of play food, a water-usable baby doll.

Say **God made everything in the world including water! God gives us water to take a bath, to wash our dishes and clothes, to play and to water plants. God is so good!**

Art

To Prepare: Craft Page 8: God Made Water; watercolor paints; brushes; large blue paper; raindrops cut from light blue paper; cotton balls; coffee filters; watercolor markers; spray bottle of water.

Have children use watercolors and brushes to paint the "God Made Water" page. Or have children scribble-color the page as their families discuss the wonderful gift of water from God.

Say **The water God makes in the raindrops is His gift to us. He gives us water in rivers, lakes, and puddles.**

Pull cotton balls apart to create clouds. Glue cotton clouds to dark blue paper. Glue light blue paper raindrop shapes to dark blue paper. Thank You, God, for making water!

Make watercolor marker "dots" on a clean coffee filter. Spritz very lightly with water from a spray bottle. Watch the watercolors blend. Hang the filters to dry on a clothesline with pinch clothespins.

Say **Thank You, God, for the water You give us to drink, to wash, to swim and the water poured over us in our Baptisms.**

Play Dough

Use blue play dough to roll and flatten rivers, lakes, and raindrops. Use white play dough to shape clouds.

Say **God makes it rain so that rivers, lakes, and oceans have water. He sends rain so plants, animals, and people have water to drink. Thank You, God, for Your gift of rain and all the water You give us!**

Discovery

To Prepare: Rain stick (purchased or homemade); wave bottle.

Before class or during, create a "wave" bottle by filling a one-liter, clear plastic bottle (label soaked off), one-third with water. Add several drops of blue food coloring. Then add about ⅓ cup colorless vegetable oil. Glue the top on securely. Use duct tape to secure the cap also. Have children wiggle and shake the bottle to make "waves" and floating colored bubbles.

Ask **Do you like to take a bubble bath? Have you had fun in a wave pool? Do you walk in the rain with Mommy and Daddy? God makes the rain and the waves. Water is an important gift from God. We couldn't live without water!**

Set out the rain stick for children to tip it upside-down to hear sounds of rain. Or make a rain stick to bring to class by filling a long cardboard tube with rice. Securely tape each end closed. Encourage children to use the rain stick and listen for the sounds of the raindrops.

Say **Thanks, God, for Your water in the world You made!**

Pretend

To Prepare: Plastic flowers; watering container; toy lawn mower; baby bottle.

Help children playact watering flowers, mowing the grass, giving a doll baby a water bottle.

Pretend to jump into the ocean or lake. Move your arms in swimming motions. Pretend to see many fish—little ones, big ones, brightly colored fish. Swim to shore, walk onto the sandy beach, shake the water off, use a towel to dry from head to toe.

Say **That was fun pretending to water the flowers! God gives us the water to use. The flowers and grass need water to grow.**

God is so good to give us the water we need in our world. What fun it is to swim! Fish wouldn't be able to live without water. Thank You, God, for the special gift of water!

Books and Puzzles

Simple shape and color puzzles; peg puzzles

Picture and board books about God's creation

Rain by Marion Dane Bauer, Sagebrush

The Lord God Made a World by Carol Greene, CPH (56-1828)

Coloring with Jesus Book 1: God Is . . . by Maria Ester de Sturtz, CPH (56-2196), a booklet of very simple creation pages for coloring or painting

Holy Baptism—Follow and Do by Joni Walker, CPH (56-2336)

Transition

While allowing time to put away Activity Center items, sing "Let's Clean Up" (CD, tracks 1, 2) and then face each other in the Singing Circle. Play "Thank the Lord and Sing His Praise" (CD, track 25) as everyone comes together.

Singing Circle

Very young children need opportunities to move their bodies and get their wiggles out. Singing Circle time is a wonderful opportunity to sing together, move to the music, wave colorful scarves or ribbons (to suggest flowing water), and do simple actions to the lyrics.

Sing **First Article Song**

Morning Prayer

All Creatures of Our God and King

1 Peter 5:7

Isaiah 43:1

Good Morning to You

Happy Birthday or **God Made Me His Child** to celebrate special occasions.

Oh, Who Can Make a Flower (Variation: "Oh, Who Can Make the Water" [or the raindrops; the rivers; the oceans; the puddles].)

He's Got the Whole World in His Hands (Variation: "He's Got the Rain and the Water in His Hands.")

God Is So Good (Variation: "God gives us rain. He's so good to us.")

2 God Speaks
10 minutes

Come to the Worship Center

Have children sit on a special rug, blanket, or quilt to get ready to hear today's Bible story. Sing or hum "Oh, Who Can Make the Water" as everyone gathers. Do action motions to show rivers or raindrops as you sing. Thank everyone for coming so nicely and for being ready to listen.

Say **In the name of the Father and of the Son and of the Holy Spirit. Amen.** Make the sign of the cross with the children.

Introducing God's Word

Sprout comes out carrying a drinking cup.

Sprout: Oh, hi, everyone! I'm so thirsty! I need a drink of water!

Teacher: Hi, Sprout! What have you been doing that made you so thirsty?

Sprout: I was playing outside with my friends, running and jumping!

Teacher: No wonder you look hot and like you need a drink of water.

Sprout: Oh, yes! I'm hot all over and my mouth is so dry.

Teacher: Here, let me pour water into your cup and help you get a drink. *(Pretend to pour water into the cup.)*

Sprout: Thank you for the drink! The water tastes so good! *(Pretends to drink from the cup.)* We couldn't live without water!

Teacher: That's right, Sprout. God's gift of water to us is so important for us to live and grow. I'm glad you came by today. Do you want to say hello to the children and their parents?

Teacher Tip
Visual aids help children to focus. Show the colorful God Made the Water Poster and the poster of Jesus' face as you tell today's Bible story.

Sprout: Oh, yes! Hi, kids! I'm glad you're here to listen to the Bible story today. *(If children are receptive to a puppet, have Sprout greet each one by name and give a little hug.)*

Teacher: You can stay and listen, too, Sprout. *(Place Sprout nearby on a table or a chair. A soup can will help to hold your puppet upright.)*

Say **Sprout needed a drink of water, didn't he? He was SO thirsty from playing outside. God gives us water to drink. You were using water a little while ago. What other things do we do with water that God gives us?** Shower or take a bath; clean our pets; water our flowers and plants; swim; clean our clothes, dishes, cars, and trucks. The pastor uses water to baptize people.

Telling God's Word

Say **Look at the poster showing the water God made for our world. God said, "Let there be water." "Let there be rain." And there was water! And there was rain!** Point to the poster of Jesus to help children visualize the name and concept of God. **God made the whole world! He made water as a special gift for His world. He makes the rivers, lakes, streams, puddles and oceans so that all the living animals and people in His world can have drinks of water, take baths, and use the water to make us feel clean and cool. God saw that it was good!**

God's gift of water is important in a special way too. God uses water to make us His dear children. Show the bowl of water, the Bible, and the seashell. Maybe when you were a baby your parents took you to church and the pastor baptized you. The pastor might have used a seashell or his hand to pour a little water on your head as he said these words (Say the following, repeating the dipping and pouring of water three times)**: [Ryan], I baptize you in the name of the Father and of the Son and of the Holy Spirit. Just like that, you belonged to God! You became His child! I'm glad to know that I was baptized and I belong to God. Are you glad too?**

Say **Wow! God gives us water for so many things! Who gives us water and rain? That's right, God does! And God saw that the water He made was good. Let's say those Bible Words and clap our hands in rhythm.**

God saw that it was good! Clap on *saw*, *it*, *good*, and then clap twice at the end. Repeat the Bible Words and clapping once or twice.

Now let's fold our hands and thank God for the water He gives us.

Say very short echo-style prayers when praying with very young children. Have children repeat the words of the prayer after you. Pause at the * and repeat the words with them. This can be a good model for parents to learn and follow too.

Pray
Thank You, God, for water*
Water for drinking,*
Water for washing,*
Water for fun splashing,*
Water that makes us Your children in Baptism.*
Thank You, God, for Jesus, our Savior and Friend.*
Amen.*

Teacher Tip

Be aware by looking at the family information page to see who has been baptized. If children and/or parents in your class are not yet baptized, assure them that God loves them dearly as His children. Offer to tell them more about Baptism after class. Offer to go with them to talk with your pastor about being baptized.

Teacher Tip

Children may not have had any previous experience praying. Routinely remind them to fold their hands, simply to keep their hands still.

Snack Time

Provide wet wipes for parents to clean the children's hands. Sing "Thank You, God, for This Food" (CD, track 15) as children fold their hands and learn that we thank God for the food and drink He gives us to enjoy.

Provide water to drink today as you mention we are celebrating the water God has made for us. Have parents place a few crackers on a napkin for their children to eat. Or serve blue "jigglers" in shapes of water drops as reminders of God's gift of Baptism and of raindrops.

Liturgy Link

As you move from the story corner to the snack table, sing or hum along with "Thank the Lord and Sing His Praise" on the CD (track 25). We thank and praise God for His Word—for Jesus, His Living Word—and we want to tell others that Jesus loves and cares for them too!

3 We Live
10 minutes

Growing through God's Word—Parent Talk

Children and Faith

While children eat their snacks and everyone is gathered around one large table, lead the parents through the following dialogue and questions. If you have a team leader, he or she may take the children to an area of the room to have a short playtime or to hear additional story books related to today's Bible lesson.

Read Hebrews 11:1–3. If your group is large enough to have small groups, ask pairs or trios of parents to discuss with one another.

Ask **How would you define faith?** Then look at Hebrews 11:4–12 to talk about one or two people from these verses who acted in faith and showed their faith.

Share a time when you or someone you know showed his or her faith.

Next, tell your partner about a time your child acted in faith.

For the whole group: **Faith is based on conviction. It's hard to define or point out, it cannot be touched, yet it exists in you and in your child.** Have someone read aloud 1 Corinthians 2:5. **Faith comes by the power of God, not through our own power or wisdom. We have nothing without God's grace—a free gift to us made possible when He gave Jesus to die on the cross to take our sins away. Through Jesus' death and resurrection, He gives us new life and the hope of living with Him in heaven when we die. When your parents brought you, and when you brought your child to the Sacrament of Baptism, the Holy Spirit planted faith in your heart and in the heart of your own child. God works His power through His Word. His Word is the foundation for you as you feed, nurture, and encourage the growth of your child's faith.**

What are some physical needs on which your child depends on you? Food and drink, clothing, shelter, warmth, security and a safe place, love and care to thrive.

God has also given parents the responsibility to provide for their children's spiritual needs. This begins in your home,

where, daily, you provide evidence to the faith that lives in your heart. What are some of the ways you provide for spiritual needs? Hearing God's Word, Bible stories; forgiving one another; telling each other "I love you; Jesus loves you"; sharing hugs and smiles; speaking of Jesus as our Friend and Savior.

As your child sees and hears faith through your actions and words, he or she is watching faith deposits made into a personal "bank of learning." As your child's own faith develops and grows, those faith deposits will be withdrawn—recalled from memory. Your words and actions today shape future understanding for your child. We can't do this by our own power, because we're sinful beings. The good news is that because of God's great love for us, through Jesus, we can rest in His promise not only to strengthen us for the tasks He gives us, but also to forgive us when we fail. We can experience His love and forgiveness daily, and help our children do the same.

Move from the table back to your Singing Circle area.

4 Closing
10 minutes

Songs and Prayers

Ask **What did we learn today? God's gift of water is so important for us to live! God cares for us so much! He cares for the whole world He made!** Have parents and children do the following action rhyme with you.

Say **God gives us water, lots of water.**
(Make wave motions with your hands.)
I drink it from a cup. *(Pretend to drink.)*
I wash my hands. *(Pretend to wash your hands.)*
I even wash my cup! *(Pretend to wash your cup.)*
God gives us water, lots of water!
(Make wave motions with your hands.)
It's there so I can swim. *(Pretend to swim.)*
But best of all I am baptized
(Make the sign of the cross on your forehead.)
Now I belong to Him! *(Point to the picture Jesus; hug yourself.)*

11

Ask **Who makes the water for us? That's right! God does because He cares for us.** Sing "1 Peter 5:7" (CD, track 16). **Let's thank God for making the gift of water.** Have families pray with you. Remind everyone to fold their hands and say the prayer words after you.

Pray **Dear God,***
Thank You for making water.*
Thank You for making us Your children.*
Thank You for taking good care of us!*
Thank You for Jesus, my Savior and Friend.*
Amen.*

Sing "Now It's Time to Say Good-bye" (CD, track 20)

Say Good-bye

Say **As you go home and during this week, look for water that God has made. You can say, "Thank You, God, for the gift of water."**

Take Homes

Family Page 8

Craft Page 8

Lesson 9

God Made the World— God Made Plants

Genesis 1:11–13

Key Point

We celebrate God, our maker, and all the plants He makes for us.

Connections

Bible Words
God saw that it was good. Genesis 1:10

Faith Words
God, Jesus, maker

Catechism
Apostles' Creed: First Article
I believe in God the Father Almighty, Maker of heaven and earth.

Liturgy
Thank the Lord and sing His praise; tell everyone what He has done.

Hymn
All Creatures of Our God and King (*Lutheran Worship* 436)

Materials Needed

1 Opening

Teacher Tools
- Nametags
- Teacher CD
- Craft Page 9: God Made Plants
- Reproducible Page 2

Other Supplies
- See "To Prepare" instructions for each Activity Center
- Rhythm ribbons or scarves

2 God Speaks

Teacher Tools
- Teacher CD
- Sprout Puppet
- God Made the Plants Poster

Other Supplies
- Poster of Jesus
- Crucifix
- Apple for Sprout
- Toddler Bible
- Bag of grass clippings, twig, flower, carrot
- *This Is the World That God Made* (CPH)

3 We Live

Teacher Tools
- Bible

Other Supplies
- Cut flower and leaf shapes from sturdy art paper
- Plastic straws cut in half

4 Closing

Teacher Tools
- Family Page 9

1 Opening
30 minutes

Welcome

If you have a white board or chalkboard, print today's Bible story focus "God Made Plants" for parents to see as they come into the room. Encourage parents to spend time with their children at one or more of the Activity Centers, focusing on thanking God for the variety of plants He gives us in His world.

Activity Centers

Water

To Prepare: measuring cups; small plastic drinking cups; a small funnel; a small sponge; a few plastic pieces of play food; a water-usable baby doll.

Repeat this activity from the previous lesson. Cover a table with a vinyl tablecloth and place a plastic pan with about 3 inches of water on the tablecloth.

Say **God made the whole world and He made water. God gives us water to take a bath, to wash our dishes and clothes, to play, and to water plants and flowers. God is so good! Do you help Mommy and Daddy** (or Grandma/Grandpa) **water the flowers and plants at your house?**

Encourage children to use the rain stick and review the "God Made Water" lesson.

Say **God knows what we need, and we need water to live. We thank God for the water He makes and gives us to enjoy. We thank God for washing us with water and His Word in Baptism.**

Rice

To Prepare: Cardboard tubes of varying lengths; tissue paper of various shades of green; play people figures.

Place a large plastic container holding about 3 inches of rice on a sheet or tablecloth. Parents and children will create trees and plants by stuffing tissue paper into the tubes, leaving some greenery sticking out of the top of each tube. Then "plant" the tubes in the rice to create a park or a garden. Add the people figures to pretend they are at the park to play and enjoy the beautiful world God has made.

Say **God makes real plants for us to enjoy. Some plants are great, big trees and bushes. Some plants are small like grass and flowers. God makes all the plants as gifts for us in His world. What plants do you like the best?**

Art

To Prepare: Craft Page 9: God Made Plants; stickers of flowers; Reproducible Page 2; sunflower seeds; chalk; tissues.

Families can color the "God Made Plants" paper and attach flower stickers as they talk about the many kinds of plants God has made as His gift to us in His world.

Say **Thank You, God, for making beautiful flowers, trees, and bushes.**

Use Reproducible Page 2 to provide the children with flower, stem, and leaf shapes. Give children a large background paper and glue sticks. Have parents help their children glue a flower garden onto the paper. Decorate the paper flowers by rubbing colored chalk over the blooms, and then rub the chalk with a tissue to soften the effect and blot the extra chalk dust. Print "God makes the flowers" on the paper.

Or have parents and children create one large sunflower on a background paper by gluing large yellow petals around a large center circle cut from brown or black paper. Spread craft glue thinly over the entire center circle to adhere sunflower seeds for the center of the flower. Add a large green stem and two long leaves.

Say **When God made all the different plants, He gave us these gifts for us to enjoy and use. We can eat apples, peaches, and pears from God's trees. We can eat raspberries from His bushes. We can eat strawberries from His plants. We can use the sunflower seeds from sunflower plants to feed the birds. Thank You, God, for so many good gifts from plants!**

Play Dough

To Prepare: Assorted play dough colors.

Encourage children to make trees, bushes, grass, fruits, and vegetables with the play dough.

Say **God makes many kinds of trees and flowers for us to enjoy. Did you see any flowers at your house today? What color did you see? Did you see the green grass as you walked into church? Did you see the flowers on the altar? What color are apples? Oranges? Pears?** Talk about various plants, vegetables, fruits, and flowers that the children might relate to in your area. **Thank You, God, for all the plants you make for us!**

Discovery

To Prepare: Garden soil; lima bean seeds; plastic container; plastic spoons; small flowerpots.

Cover a table with a vinyl tablecloth. Have children take turns pouring spoons of planting soil into small plastic flowerpots within a low-sided plastic container to catch the soil. When their pots are filled within an inch of the top, show them how to use their index finger to push two lima bean seeds into the soil. Sprinkle with water.

Say **Thank You, God, for the soil, the water, and the sunshine to help the bean seeds grow. We'll watch our seeds in the pots. What surprise do you think we'll see?**

Pretend

To Prepare: Plastic flowers; watering can; toy lawn mower; pretend items.

Use plastic gardening tools and wear small gardening gloves. Encourage children to pretend to garden with their parents. Plant seeds, pick flowers or tomatoes, put peas or corn into a pan to cook for lunch.

Say **We can plants seeds and small plants to grow in a garden. God makes the flowers and vegetables grow. He sends the rain and the sunshine for the plants. What are some of the plants that we can eat to help us grow? God is so good! We thank God for trees, flowers, fruits and vegetables, and grass too!**

Say the action rhyme and have families do the actions together:

Teacher Tip
Many very young children like to sit with their parents and look at colorful picture books and work on simple wooden or foam puzzles that have shapes and colors.

Say **Once there was a seed in the dark, dark ground.**
(Hide finger in fist of other hand.)
God made the sun shine so big and round.
(Make big "sun" circle with arms.)
Down came the rain so gentle and slow.
(Wiggle fingers from high to low.)
Up came the little seed—grow, grow, grow!
(Push finger through fist.)

Books and Puzzles

Provide books and puzzles on a separate table or on a corner of your main Activity Center table. Focus on today's Bible story, God Made Plants.

Transition

Play the CD songs "Let's Clean Up," "1 Peter 5:7," and "Thank the Lord and Sing His Praise" as families help put away Activity Center items (CD, tracks 1, 2, 21, and 25).

Singing Circle

As you sing today, wave colorful scarves or ribbons to remind everyone of flowing water. Do simple actions to the lyrics when appropriate.

Sing **First Article Song**

Morning Prayer

All Creatures of Our God and King

1 Peter 5:7

Isaiah 43:1

Good Morning to You

Happy Birthday or **God Made Me His Child** to celebrate special occasions.

Oh, Who Can Make a Flower (Review the verse "Oh, Who Can Make the Water" today and add the new verse "Oh, Who Can Make a Flower" and "Oh, Who Can Make a Tree.")

He's Got the Whole World in His Hands (Variation: "He's Got the Rain and the Water in His Hands" and "He's Got the Trees and the Flowers in His Hands.")

God Is So Good (Lyrics: "God Made the Plants")

2 God Speaks
10 minutes

Come to the Worship Center

16

Have children sit in front of your altar to get ready to hear today's Bible story. Sing or hum "Oh, Who Can Make the Water" (CD, track 16) as everyone gathers. Do action motions to show rivers or raindrops as you sing.

Say **I'm so glad you're here!** Welcome each child by name. **I'm happy you came to learn about God, our maker, and how much He cares for you!** Point to the poster of Jesus. **We thank God for the best gift of all—Jesus—who died on the cross for us and came alive again!** Hold up a poster of Jesus or have a crucifix on your altar.

Introducing God's Word

Sprout comes in carrying an apple.

Sprout: Look, [teacher's name], I brought something for a snack today!

Teacher: Hi, Sprout! That looks like a yummy apple. Where did you get it?

Sprout: Daddy bought it at the grocery store. Do apples grow in the store?

Teacher: No, Sprout! Apples don't grow in a grocery store. Boys and girls, do you know where apples grow? *(Listen to answers, encourage parents to participate, and then say,)* Yes! Apples grow on beautiful apple trees!

Sprout: Wow! Where do the apple trees grow?

Teacher: Apple trees are plants. God made apple trees. *(Open the precut apple to show the seeds.)* Each apple has tiny seeds inside it. If we plant the seeds in the soil and they get just the right amount of sunshine, rain, and food in the soil, the seeds will grow into apple trees.

Sprout: Then I can pick apples for the girls and boys to have a snack!

Teacher: Well, Sprout, it takes a long, long time for apple seeds to grow into trees and then for the trees to have apples on them.

Sprout: Then I'll just get apples from Daddy and Mommy! Don't you love the way an apple crunches and tastes so good?

Teacher: Yes, Sprout. God gives us apples to help keep our bodies healthy. Enjoy your apple snack. Thanks for coming by! We'll see you next time!

Tell the Bible Story

Hold up the apple again, and point to the apple trees in today's poster.

Say **God makes apple trees and many other fruits and vegetables for us to eat. These are all God's gifts to us in His world that He made. God takes good care of us, doesn't He?**

God said, "Let there be trees. Let there be flowers. Let there be fruits and vegetables. And let there be grass!" And as soon as He said the words, there were trees, flowers, fruits and vegetables, and grass! Point to the poster of Jesus to help children visualize the name and concept of God. **God loves His world so much. He made plants of all kinds. And God saw that it was good!**

Ask **What is in this bag?** Hold up the bag of grass clippings. **God makes the green grass for you to run and play and roll on.**

Hold up the twig. **God makes trees grow sturdy and tall to give you shade and to keep you cool in the hot sunshine.**

Show the flower. **God makes beautiful flowers and plants for you to see and smell.**

Hold up the carrot. **God makes carrots and other vegetables for you to eat to help you grow big and strong.**

Who gives us many kinds of plants? That's right, God does! And God saw that the plants He made were good. Let's say those Bible Words and clap our hands in rhythm.

God saw that it was good! Repeat the Bible Words activity from the previous lesson. Clap on *saw*, *it*, *good*, and then clap twice at the end. Repeat the Bible Words, clapping once or twice.

Now let's fold our hands and thank God for the plants He gives.

Liturgy Link

Listen to "Thank the Lord and Sing His Praise" on the CD (track 25). Sing or hum along a few times as everyone moves from the story corner to the snack table.

Say this echo-style prayer. Pause at the * and repeat the words with the children.

Pray **Thank You, God, for trees.***
Thank You, God, for grass.*
Thank You, God, for flowers.*
Thank You, God, for apples and carrots.*
Thank You, God, for Jesus, our Savior and Friend.*
Amen.*

Snack Time

15

Provide wipes for cleaning the children's hands; provide water to drink.

Sing "Thank You, God, for This Food" (CD, track 15) as children fold their hands and thank God for the food and drink He gives us to enjoy.

Say **We thank God for the water God has made for us!**

Have parents place a few cookies or apple slices on a napkin for their children.

Alternative Flowerpot Snack: Following the directions below, create a flower planted in a flowerpot for today's snack. Ask parents to help their children sprinkle cookie crumbs on top of an opened pudding cup. This represents the potting soil in which we plant seeds and plants. Children may then stick a straw holding a flower into the pudding to "plant the flower." Finally, add a gummy worm to the "soil." Explain that God gives us worms to keep the soil full of vitamins and oxygen and air holes. Provide napkins to place the flowers on while eating.

Read a short picture book about plants while children eat. Suggestions include: *The Carrot Seed* by Ruth Krauss and *The Tiny Seed* by Eric Carle.

3 We Live
10 minutes

Growing through God's Word—Parent Talk

Model Faith for Your Child

While children eat their snacks, lead the parents through the following dialogue and questions. If you have a team leader, he or she may take the children to hear a related Bible story.

Ask **What is faith? Where does faith come from?** Have the group share thoughts.

Read Hebrews 11:1 and Romans 10:17.

Say **We doubt that God will provide what we need even though we confess in the Catechism that "He richly and daily provides me with all that I need for this body and life." Our sinful nature causes us to doubt, not believe. It causes us to question, not trust. Through His Word and Sacrament, God's Holy Spirit works in our hearts and minds. God promises us that "if you confess with your mouth, that Jesus is Lord and believe in your heart that God raised Him from the dead, you will be saved" (Romans 10:9). What good news! We can't "grow faith" by ourselves. We can't save ourselves from sin either. But we can rejoice that God has made it all possible for us through the work of His Son, Jesus. God's free gift of forgiveness belongs to us and to our children because of Jesus' death and resurrection. The third person of the Trinity, the Holy Spirit, works faith in our hearts so that we live a faith-filled life as God's children and demonstrate our love and forgiveness toward others. Faith is a gift from God!**

What are some things you could do at home to show your faith? What are things that people say and do that do not give evidence to faith and may even harm the growth of faith? Have parents read Romans 10:17, then discuss what God says to us.

Say **In addition to showing your faith by words and actions at home, what else can you do to help your child's faith grow? Name times and places when and where your child can hear God's Word. How can you use these times and places to help you in your responsibility as a Christian parent?**

Others see evidence of our faith in our hope, joy, love, and peace. When your child sees hugs, smiles, and a willingness to help others, he or she sees evidence of faith. When your child hears words of encouragement and forgiveness, your child hears faith.

Second to God's Word, YOU have the greatest impact on your child. What you say and do serve as examples. Your children watch and listen to you and learn how to respond in various situations. They will treat others as you treat them. They will handle anger as you do. They will watch you pray, read your Bible, worship, and sing and model your actions. They will forgive as you forgive and ask to be forgiven.

Likewise, when your son sees you fretting about your health, money, or other needs, as if it all were up to you, he learns a lesson that you don't want him to learn!

If your daughter falls and scrapes her knee, what can you do right then and there to focus on Jesus and His care? Say a short prayer such as, "Dear Jesus, please help [Tiffany's] scraped knee get better quickly. We know you love her. Amen."

When your child takes a toy away from a play friend, or the opposite happens, how will you respond? Help parents role-play the situation. Remind them to direct the child to say "I'm sorry" and to share. Always remind a child, "I didn't like what you did, but I always love you."

Even the youngest of children need to hear God's Word and

about His love and care for us. They can hear how God makes the rain to fall, the sun to shine in the daytime, the plants to grow for food. They can hear bedtime, mealtime, and even between-time prayers. They especially need to hear about their Savior, Jesus, who died on the cross for them. Think about and deliberately choose your words and actions as you model faith.

Move from the table back to your Singing Circle area.

4 Closing
10 minutes

Songs and Prayers

16, 17

Ask **What did we learn today?** Sing "Oh, Who Can Make a Flower" (CD, tracks 16, 17) and sing each verse as you pass around the items used in storytelling today.

God is so good to us. He made plants to give us food, to give us shade, and to make our world beautiful! What wonderful gifts He gives us! Let's clap our Bible Words again: God saw that it was good!

Who makes the plants for us? That's right! God does, because He cares for us. Let's thank God for giving us plants. Have families pray with you. Remind everyone to fold their hands and say the prayer words after you.

Pray **Dear God,***
Thank You for giving us plants.*
Thank You for all Your gifts in our world.*
Thank You for taking good care of me!*
Thank You for Jesus, our Savior and Friend.*
Amen.*

Sing "Now It's Time to Say Good-bye" (CD, track 20)

20

Say Good-bye

Say **When you see beautiful flowers and trees and grass, thank God for taking good care of you! Thank Him for sending Jesus to be Your Savior!**

Take Homes

Family Page 9

Craft Page 9

Lesson 10

God Made the World—God Made the Sun, Moon, and Stars

Genesis 1:14–19

Key Point

We celebrate God, our maker, and the sun, moon, and stars He made for the world

Connections

Bible Words
God saw that it was good. Genesis 1:10

Faith Words
God, Jesus, maker

Catechism
Apostles' Creed: First Article
I believe in God the Father Almighty, Maker of heaven and earth.

Liturgy
Thank the Lord and sing His praise; tell everyone what He has done.

Hymn
All Creatures of Our God and King (*Lutheran Worship* 436)

Materials Needed

1 Opening

Teacher Tools
- Nametags
- Teacher CD
- Craft Page 10: God Made the Sun, Moon, and Stars
- Reproducible Page 3

Other Supplies
- See "To Prepare" section for each Activity Center
- Large white and yellow balloons
- Ribbons, 24 inches long

2 God Speaks

Teacher Tools
- Sprout Puppet
- God Made the Sun, Moon, and Stars Poster

Other Supplies
- Poster of Jesus
- Sunglasses for puppet
- Toddler Bible
- *This Is the World That God Made* (CPH)

3 We Live

Teacher Tools
- Bible

4 Closing

Teacher Tools
- Family Page 10
- God Made the Sun, Moon, and Stars Poster

1 Opening
30 minutes

Welcome

Print today's Bible story focus "God Made the Sun, Moon, and Stars" on your white board for parents to see as they come into the room. Point out the main theme for today.

Encourage parents to spend time with their children at one or more of the Activity Centers, focusing on thanking God for the gifts of the sun, moon, and stars.

Activity Centers

Water

To Prepare: Rain sticks; plastic dolls; cups; play food.

Repeat the water-play activities to reinforce the previous lessons. Cover a table with a vinyl tablecloth and place a plastic pan containing about three inches of water on the tablecloth. Provide measuring cups, small plastic drinking cups, a small funnel, a small sponge, a few plastic pieces of play food, or a water-usable baby doll.

Ask **What are some ways we use water? God is so good! We have water to drink, to wash our bodies, to brush our teeth, and to clean our dishes. Do you help Daddy or Mommy wash your car or your dog? Do you give your cat a drink of water? Sprinkle the flowers and gardens and grass at your house? God gives us water for many things! Water keeps us alive. We were baptized with water and God's Word. Water is God's gift!**

Encourage children to use the rain stick and review the "God Made Water" lesson.

Say **God knows what we need, and we need water to live. We thank God for the water He makes.**

Rice

To Prepare: Rice in a pan; cardboard tubes; green tissue paper; play people figures.

Young children need much repetition. They enjoy doing the same activities over and over. Set a large plastic container holding a few inches of rice on a sheet or tablecloth. Parents and children may make tissue paper and cardboard tube shrubs, trees, and plants and set them into the rice to make a garden or a park.

Say **God makes great big trees and small shrubs. God makes all the plants. Let's make a beautiful park and plant the trees and bushes in our rice pan today. Thank You, God, for all the plants and flowers You make and give to us to enjoy!**

Art

To Prepare: Craft Page 10: God Made the Sun, Moon, and Stars; stickers of sun, moon, and stars; paint smocks; large, dark blue background paper; yellow tempera paint; white tempera paint; sunshine stamp; moon and stars stamp; two pans for paint (pie tins or plastic lids); shiny star stickers; Reproducible Page 3.

Say **We thank God for His gift of the sun, moon and stars to us.**

As children color Craft Page10, talk about what gives us light in the daytime and what gives us light and shines at night. Add stars, sun, and moon stickers.

Provide large, dark construction paper for the background of today's project. Supply markers so that parents can print their children's names in the corner of the paper. Have them print "Thank You, God, for the sun, moon, and stars" across the top or bottom of the papers too.

You'll want to have parents paint with their children at the very beginning of today's session to allow time for the paint to dry.

Place a small amount of yellow paint in one of the paint pans (an aluminum pie tin or a large plastic lid).

Load a small amount of yellow paint onto the sunshine stamp.

Say **Hold your child's hand as you stamp the sunshine one or more times. Thank You, God, for making the sun to keep us warm.**

Place a small amount of white paint in the second paint pan. Use the white paint and the moon and stars stamp next.

Say **Again, hold your child's hand as you stamp the moon and stars. Thank You, God, for making the moon to give us light at night. And for making the beautiful stars to shine in the night sky.**

Or use Reproducible Page 3 to provide each child with a yellow paper circle and a white paper circle or crescent moon shape. Parents will help children attach the sun and moon shapes and sparkly star stickers to their dark paper.

Play Dough

Parents and children can make the yellow sun and white moon and stars.

Ask **Did you see the sun shining in the sky today? I'm glad God made the sun to warm us and help the flowers and trees grow.**

When you go to bed tonight, look for the moon and the stars in the night sky. Sometimes the moon looks like a big ball. Sometimes it looks like a little crescent cookie.

Count the stars you see. Do they twinkle? We thank God for the sun, moon, and stars He made for us!

Discovery

To Prepare: Dark blue or black construction paper; star punch; flashlight; stars cut from poster board.

Place a flashlight and the "star finder" on a corner of your table. After cutting stars in the paper, parents can show their children how to hold the dark paper and shine the flashlight from one side so that the stars appear on a wall or on the ceiling.

Say **Look at all the stars! God made the stars! They shine and remind us how much God loves us and takes care of us.**

Put 5–10 sturdy yellow or white stars cut from poster board into a basket on the corner of your table. Encourage parents and children to hide a star and then find it.

Say **Thank You, God, for making stars!**

If the sun is shining brightly today, stand near a glass door or window and feel the warmth of the sun. Or take a few minutes to walk outside if possible. Look at the shadows, move around, and watch the shadows move too. If the sun isn't shining, remind children that the clouds sometimes hide the sun. But we know the sun is still there because God gives us light. If it is available, consider walking into the church to see how the sun shines through the church's windows.

Say **God gives us the sun in the sky for daytime and the moon and the stars for night lights. Isn't God good?**

Pretend

To Prepare: Beach blanket or large sheet; sunglasses; sand toys; large yellow balloon; pillow; blanket; stuffed animal or baby doll; yard toys.

Parents and children can pretend they are at the beach, spread a blanket, play with sand toys and feel the warm sunshine (the yellow balloon hung in this area).

Say **We have fun playing outside and going to the lake (or pool) on a warm, sunny day. Wiggle your toes in the warm sand! Wear your sunglasses to protect your eyes. Pretend that we're putting sunscreen on so we don't burn our skin.**

Pretend it's nighttime. Gather your pillow, blanket and favorite stuffed animal or baby doll. Say a nighttime prayer. Then pretend to look out the window. **What does God put into the sky at night? Let's tell our babies, "God will watch over you while you sleep." Thank You, God, for the moon and stars and for watching over us.**

Pretend as you use the plastic yard toys—rake, lawnmower, garden gloves, sprinkling can. Talk about how special and important it is to take care of the gifts in God's world and to enjoy the sunshine He gives us.

Books and Puzzles

Provide simple shape puzzles and books on a table or on a blanket in a corner of your room. Favorites include these public library books:

Apostles' Creed—Follow and Do by Joni Walker, CPH (56-2336)

Goodnight Moon by Margaret Wise Brown, HarperFestival, 1991

Good Night Sun, Hello Moon by Karen Viola, Reader's Digest, 2004

Transition

1, 2

Ring a bell, begin to play the clean-up song. Sing "Let's Clean Up" (CD, tracks 1, 2) and move to your Singing Circle.

Singing Circle

Have children wave a big yellow or white balloon by holding the ribbon loop.

Say **The balloons can remind us of the sun and the moon God puts in the sky.**

Sing **First Article Song**

Morning Prayer

All Creatures of Our God and King

1 Peter 5:7

Isaiah 43:1

Good Morning to You

Happy Birthday or **God Made Me His Child** to celebrate special occasions.

Oh, Who Can Make a Flower (Variation: "Oh, Who Can Make the Sunshine" and "Oh, Who Can Make the Moon and Stars." Make a circle with your hands above your head for the sunshine. Make a smaller circle with your hands in front of you for the moon. Wiggle your fingers like twinkling stars.)

He's Got the Whole World in His Hands (Variation: "He's Got the Sun and the Stars in His Hands.")

God Is So Good (Variation: "God makes the sun . . . God makes the moon . . . God makes the stars.")

Jesus in the Morning (Praise Him, Praise Him)

Use a Sharpie pen to make a happy face on one side and a sleeping face on the opposite side of a paper plate. Show the happy face side as you sing about the morning, move the plate to "noontime" above your head, and then turn the plate to show the sleeping face and move it slowly down to the opposite side as if the sun is setting as you sing about the sun going down. (Consider premaking one for each child to use as you sing this song together.) Save the visuals to use another time.

2 God Speaks
10 minutes

Come to the Worship Center

3

Play "All Creatures of Our God and King" (CD, track 3) as families gather.

Say **I'm so glad you're here!** Welcome each child by name. **I'm happy you came to hear how much God loves you!** Point to the poster of Jesus. **Jesus is always with us. He cares for you and me. That makes us happy! Now we will begin our lesson for today.**

In the name of the Father and of the Son and of the Holy Spirit. Amen. As you say these holy words, encourage the children to say them with you while making the sign of the cross.

Introducing God's Word

Sprout comes in wearing sunglasses. If the sun isn't shining today, have Sprout hold the sunglasses and talk about what he likes to do when the sun *is* shining or things he can do when it's cloudy or rainy outside.

Sprout: Hooray! Hooray! The sun is shining! Hooray!

Teacher: Hi, Sprout! You sound happy.

Sprout: I am! I like it when the sun shines!

Teacher: What do you like to do on a sunny day?

Sprout: I like to play outside with my friends. I like to ride my bike the best!

Teacher: We're so glad God made the sun shine in the sky. The sun is one of God's gifts to us!

Sprout: Yes! The sun makes us warm. Sometimes it makes us HOT!

Teacher: That's right, Sprout. And did you know that God made the moon and stars to shine at night?

Sprout: Yes! God is so great! Do you ever see the moon and the stars when you look out your window, girls and boys? I do!

Teacher: God is so good to give us the day and the night lights in the sky.

Sprout: I'm going to keep my sunglasses on today. I'm going to play with my friends now. See you next time!

Teacher: Have fun in God's sunshine, Sprout! Bye!

Telling God's Word

Say Hold the Bible open as you say, **God's book, the Bible, tells us that God made the sun, the moon, and the stars.**

19

God's Word is written down. It's really true. We thank God for the Bible! Sing "Written Down" (CD, track 19).

Now let's close our eyes. Is it dark? Keep your eyes closed. Once it was very, very dark. There was no sun, and no moon or stars either. There was only God. And God said, "Let there be light." And then there was light!

Open your eyes. Is the light bright? When God made the sunshine, it was bright too!

God made the sun and put it into the sky to shine during the day. Point to the sun on the poster for today.

God made the moon and stars and put them into the sky.

The sun, moon, and stars all remind us how much God loves us and takes care of us! Point to the sun, moon, and stars on the poster.

When God made the sun, the moon, and the stars, God saw that it was good! Let's say those Bible Words and clap our hands.

God saw that it was good! Repeat the Bible Words activity from the previous lesson. Clap on *saw*, *it*, *good*, and then clap twice at the end.

Now let's fold our hands and thank God for the sun, moon, and stars He gives us. Have children repeat the words of the prayer after you. Pause at the * and repeat the words with them.

Pray

Thank You, God, for the sunshine.*
Thank You, God, for the moon.*
Thank You, God, for the stars.*
Thank You for making the whole world!*
We love You, God.*
Amen.*

Say **God made so many good gifts for us when He made the world. We want to thank and praise Him and tell others about His love for us!**

Snack Time

15

Provide wet wipes. Sing "Thank You, God, for This Food" (CD, track 15).

If children enjoy round crackers and cookies or round fruit sections today, remind them God, our maker, gave us the round sunshine and the moon in the sky. Crescent-shaped cookies remind us of the part of the moon we sometimes see at night.

Say **Thank You, God, for Your good gifts!**

Alternative snack: Jell-O jigglers in circle and star shapes

Liturgy Link

Sing "Thank the Lord and Sing His Praise" as you make the transition from the story corner to the snack table.

3 We Live
10 minutes

Growing through God's Word—Parent Talk

Children and Trust

Lead parents through the following dialogue and questions.

Ask someone to read Psalm 9:10 and 22:8.

Say **It is a given that we trust the sun to rise and the moon and stars to appear each night. Yet do we ever stop to consider who or what we trust for these daily miracles of nature? It is because of the sacrifice of our Savior, Jesus, that the whole world receives such daily provision from our heavenly Father. Without Christ, all creation would be in utter chaos, completely broken by sin. When we understand how God cares for us even when we don't ask or think about it, we begin to understand how great His loving care is! Let's remember some of the ways God has met His people's needs when they have called to Him.** Ask parents to share Bible stories in which they remember someone needing God's help: the Israelites in Egypt, in the wilderness; Daniel in the lion's den; three men in the fiery furnace; Mary and Joseph escaping from Herod. **The people trusted God because He gave them care, food, water, safety, and love.**

Let's list needs that we've had during our lives. Use a chart or white board to write the group's suggestions. If necessary, lead them to identify the spiritual needs we have as sinful beings. **Imagine you and your child being separated by a locked door. Your child cries and needs your comfort. But he or she can't unlock the door to get to you. What despair! Each of us adults are that very young, crying child, separated from the loving parent, who is God, our Father. We can't unlock the door to get to Him. We're sinful. We have no key. We can't save ourselves. The key that unlocks the door so that we can come to our heavenly Father is His Son, our Savior, Jesus! When He died on the cross to take the sins of the world away, He unlocked the door and knocked down the barrier separating us from God and His welcoming arms. Jesus took care of our greatest need—that of forgiveness. It's the same for children of all ages. Our greatest need is forgiveness of our sins. God knew the needs of all people since Adam and Eve sinned for the first time. He kept His promise and He provided for our needs in His only Son, the best gift of all time.**

When your child was an infant, what basic needs did you meet for him or her, and how?

How did God bless the people as they learned to put their trust in Him? Read Psalm 37:3–5. **How do children benefit from being able to trust the adults in their lives?**

When your child experiences your loving care at times of his or her needs—feedings, diaper changes, playtime, rocking, and cuddling—trust develops. When might a child lose trust? Promises made aren't kept; mixed messages are given—we don't practice what we preach; our loving words aren't backed by loving actions. **How can we restore trust?** Give honest answers to questions; ask for forgiveness; show Jesus' love in words and actions.

When you help your child develop trust in you, you lay the foundation for him or her to trust in our loving God.

Move from the table back to your Singing Circle area.

4 Closing
10 minutes

Songs and Prayers

17, 3

Ask **What did we learn today?** Sing "Oh, Who Can Make the Sunshine?" and "Oh, Who Can Make the Moon and Stars?" (CD, track 17) as you point to the God Made the Sun, Moon, and Stars Poster. Sing, "All Creatures of Our God and King" (CD, track 3).

God is so good to us. He makes the sun shine, the moon, and the stars to light our world. Let's clap our Bible Words again: God saw that it was good!

Who made the sun, moon, and stars for us? That's right! God gave us those gifts. See how much He cares for us! Let's thank God. Have families pray with you.

Pray

Dear God,*
Thank You for making the sun,*
For making the moon,*
And for making the stars.*
We love You!*
Amen.*

20

Sing "Now It's Time to Say Good-bye" (CD, track 20)

Say Good-bye

Say **When you see the sun, moon, and stars, you can say "Thank You, God, for loving me!"**

Take Homes

Family Page 10

Craft Page 10

Lesson 11

God Made the World— God Made Sea Creatures

Genesis 1:20–21

Key Point

We thank and praise God for all the sea creatures He made in His world.

Connections

Bible Words
God saw that it was good. Genesis 1:10

Faith Words
God, Jesus, maker

Catechism
Apostles' Creed: First Article
I believe in God the Father Almighty, Maker of heaven and earth.

Liturgy
Thank the Lord and sing His praise; tell everyone what He has done.

Hymn
All Creatures of Our God and King (*Lutheran Worship* 436)

Materials Needed

1 Opening

Teacher Tools

- Nametags
- Teacher CD
- Craft Page 11: God Made the Sea Creatures
- Reproducible Page 4

Other Supplies

- See "To Prepare" instructions for each Activity Center
- Ribbons or scarves (blues/greens to represent water/waves)

2 God Speaks

Teacher Tools

- Teacher CD
- Sprout Puppet
- God Made the Sea Creatures Poster

Other Supplies

- Poster of Jesus
- Toddler Bible
- *This Is the World That God Made* (CPH)
- Five fish shapes cut from felt
- Flannel board
- Pictures of a whale, a dolphin, a sea horse, an octopus, and children, backed with felt

3 We Live

Teacher Tools

- Bible

4 Closing

Teacher Tools

- Family Page 11
- *This Is the World That God Made* (CPH)

1 Opening
30 minutes

Welcome

Print today's Bible story focus "God Made Sea Creatures" on your white board. Remind parents that they will want to reinforce the Bible truth with their children during Activity Center time and throughout the new week.

Encourage parents to spend time with their children at one or more of the Activity Centers, focusing on thanking God for the many different sea creatures He has made and takes care of for us.

Activity Centers

Water

To Prepare: Plastic or foam fish shapes; pinch-style clothespins.

Cover your water center with a vinyl tablecloth. Place plastic or foam fish (precut shapes) and pinch clothespins near the water pan.

Float the fish on the water. Show children how to squeeze open the clothespins to "catch" the fish. Place the fish into a basket or other small container.

Say **Thank You, God, for making fish. Thank You, God, for my fingers that can squeeze and catch the fish. The fish You made are gifts to us!**

Teacher Tip

Cover the rice pan area with a vinyl tablecloth or a large sheet. After children finish with this center, it's easy to pour the rice back into the container and put the lid on it.

Rice

To Prepare: Sponge fish and sea creature shapes; seashells.

Place fish, starfish, octopus, and whale shapes cut from sponges near the rice pan. Add seashells to this center too.

Have children hide the sea creatures and shells in the rice and find each item.

Say **God made each sea creature different. Thank You, God, for the starfish . . . for the octopus . . . for the whale . . . for the fish You made. Thank You for the beautiful gifts of sea creatures!**

Art

To Prepare: Craft Page 11: God Made the Sea Creatures; fish stickers; paint smocks; large white paper; watercolor paints and large brushes; self-stick art foam sea creature shapes; Reproducible Page 4.

Say **When God made creatures that live in oceans and rivers, He said "It is good!" Sea creatures are God's gifts to us. God made the whole world!**

Talk about the many different sea creatures as children paint (or scribble-color) the "God Made Sea Creatures" page and add fish stickers today.

Provide large white paper for the children's art project background. Print "God makes sea creatures" across the bottom of the paper. Add the child's name before beginning the project. Have paint smocks for children to wear while they use the watercolor paints. Parents can help children use a large brush to watercolor waves and water into the bottom half of their paper. They might add a sun and clouds to the sky also.

Say **Look at the waves you've made! God made the water. Then He made sea creatures to live in the oceans, lakes, rivers, ponds, and streams.**

When your art paper is dry, you'll add sea creatures to your picture. Can you think of things that live in water? Thank You, God, for the water and sea creatures You made!

Put children's papers in a safe place to dry. After the paint is dry, before class is over, give each child a number of sea creatures made from art foam (fish, octopus, clam, lobster, dolphin, whale, starfish—all available in craft stores) to attach to the watercolor page. Parents will need to help peel the back off each to stick the items to the paper.

Or use Reproducible Page 4 to give each child a set of precut paper sea creatures. Parents can help children use glue sticks to attach their sea creatures to their wave papers.

Play Dough

To Prepare: Play dough in assorted colors; marker; paper plates; plastic knives; cookie cutters of sea creatures.

Before class, use a marker to draw a generic fish outline onto several paper plates. Draw a clamshell, a whale, a turtle, and other sea creatures as desired, one per paper plate. Encourage children to press one color of play dough onto a fish shape, another color onto a shell shape, and so on.

Children can use plastic knives to cut small pieces of play dough and press the pieces onto a fish pattern to create spots on the fish.

Ask **Do you have fish in an aquarium at home? God makes fish so colorful and beautiful! I like the way you've made a blue-spotted fish! Thank You, God, for all Your colorful fish and sea creatures. They are gifts from You to us!**

Parents can help children use star- and fish-shaped cookie cutters to make play dough sea creatures.

Discovery

To Prepare: clean sand; magnifying glass with handle; assortment of seashells, urchins, starfish, and sand dollars (can be purchased at a craft/hobby store).

If possible, bring a plastic container of white beach sand or clean sand. Place seashells, starfish, clamshells, sand dollars, and sea urchin shells in the container.

Ask **Which shell is the biggest? The smallest? The smoothest? The roughest?**

Add a magnifying glass with a handle to allow children to see the sea creatures closely.

Pretend

To Prepare: Large fish shapes cut from sturdy paper; large paper clips; plastic or wooden magnetic fishing "poles"; hula-hoop or masking tape; small plastic frying pan.

Before class, cut large fish shapes from colorful construction paper or poster board. Attach a large paper clip to the mouth of each paper fish. Tie yarn to one end of a dowel rod or plastic fishing pole. Tie a magnet to the end of the fishing yarn. Have two fishing poles if you have more than four children in class. Use a hula-hoop to create a fishing pond on the floor or mark a lake area by using masking tape. Place the fish inside the area.

Children catch the fish by dangling the fishing pole until the magnet touches a paper clip on a fish.

Say **Put the caught fish into a basket. When all the fish are caught, pretend to fry the fish in a pan. Fish are fun to catch, and fish are so good to eat! Thank You, God, for giving us fish!**

Books and Puzzles

Provide simple shape puzzles and books on a table or on a blanket in a corner of your room.

A wooden magnetic fish and fishing pole puzzle set might be available in a local teachers' store. Children use a pole with a small magnet on the end to place fish into the puzzle shapes.

Cut matching fish shapes from bright colors of felt. (Two red fish, two blue fish, two green fish and so on.) Have children place the matching fish together on a large flannel board.

Apostles' Creed—Follow and Do by Joni Walker, CPH (56-2336)

Baby Senses: Touch by Susanna Beaumont, Make Believe Ideas, 2005 (This book has touch opportunities and colorful illustrations for a bumpy starfish, a rough clamshell, as well as a furry lion, kitten, and sheep to touch.)

Teacher Tip

Let your pastor or church music director know that the children have been learning the hymn, "All Creatures of Our God and King" as well as "Thank the Lord and Sing His Praise" (CD, tracks 3 and 25). Perhaps they will look for an appropriate time to sing the hymn in an upcoming worship service. The children will be thrilled to sing this hymn with all the people in church!

Transition

Alert families that they have a few minutes to put activity items away. Then come to the Singing Circle. Play favorite songs on the CD and sing along.

Singing Circle

Have children wave flowing blue and green ribbons or scarves to represent water and waves.

Sing **First Article Song**

Morning Prayer

All Creatures of Our God and King

1 Peter 5:7

Isaiah 43:1

Good Morning to You

Happy Birthday or **God Made Me His Child** to celebrate special occasions.

Oh, Who Can Make a Flower (Variation: "Oh, Who Can Make the Fish Swim." Move your hands together as a fish would wriggle through the water.)

He's Got the Whole World in His Hands (Variation: "He's Got the Fish and the Whales in His Hands.")

God Is So Good (Variation: God makes the fish; God makes the shells; God makes the whales.)

Jesus in the Morning (Praise Him, Praise Him) (Use the paper plate visual again. Children like repetition!)

2 God Speaks
10 minutes

Come to the Worship Center

17, 13

Play "Oh, Who Can Make a Flower" (CD, track 17) as parents and children gather and sit on a special rug or blanket. Sing softly with the music.

Say **Come and sit with me. I'm so glad you're here!** Welcome each child by name. **I'm happy you came to hear how much God loves and cares for you!** Point to the poster of Jesus. **Jesus is always with us. He cares for us! That makes us happy!** Do the action verse "Open Them, Close Them" (CD, track 13). **Now let's say the special words that start our lesson. Can you say them with me and make the sign of the cross?**

In the name of the Father and of the Son and of the Holy Spirit. Amen.

Introducing God's Word

Sprout comes humming "Oh, Who Can make a Flower" happily.

Sprout: Hi, everybody! Guess what I did this morning!

Teacher: Hmm, did you eat ten pancakes?

Sprout: No, don't be silly!

Teacher: Did you put your shoes on backwards?

Sprout: No, you're being silly again!

Teacher: I give up. Sprout, tell us what you did.

Sprout: I fed my cousin's pet fish!

Teacher: That's great, Sprout! You helped take care of one of God's sea creatures.

Sprout: My cousin's fish lives in a fish bowl. Do all God's sea creatures live in a bowl?

Teacher: No, Sprout. God made some fish to live in fresh water like lakes or rivers. Other creatures live in salt water, the ocean, like whales, dolphins, and sharks.

Sprout: Wow! God made a lot of sea creatures!

Teacher: Yes, He did, Sprout! He made sharks and sea horses, water snakes and turtles, big fish and little fish. And do you know what the best part is?

Sprout: What's the best part?

Teacher: God takes care of all His sea creatures, and He takes care of you and me!

Sprout: I'm going to tell my cousin about all the sea creatures. Maybe we can look at books about all the sea creatures God has made. Bye, everybody!

Teacher: Bye, Sprout!

Telling God's Word

Say Hold the Toddler Bible open as you say, **God's book, the Bible, tells us that God made all the creatures that live in the water. They are God's gifts to us. He made the whole world!**

God's Word is written down. It's really true. We thank God for the Bible! Sing "Written Down" (CD, track 19) to help children grow to learn that God's Word is very special and true and we thank Him for it.

Show the God Made the Sea Creatures Poster and/or the page in the big book for today. Ask children to point to the whale, dolphin, sea horse, and so on.

Then place five felt fish cutouts on a flannel board. As you say each of the following verses (2–6) and point to each fish, ask a child to add the felt-backed picture (or sea creature shape in art foam) to the flannel board.

Say **Five little fish swimming in the sea.**
God made the fish and God made me. *(Point to yourself.)*

The first fish said, "Whales swim with me."
"God made the whales and God made me." *(Add the whale.)*

The second fish said, "Dolphins swim with me."
"God made the dolphins and God made me." *(Add the dolphin.)*

The third fish said, "Sea horses swim with me."
"God made the sea horse and God made me." *(Add the sea horse.)*

The fourth fish said, "Octopuses swim with me."
"God made the octopus and God made me." *(Add the octopus.)*

The fifth fish said, "Children swim with me."
"God made the children and God made me." *(Point to the children.)*

Have children find the fish, whales, dolphins, sea horses, and octopuses in the poster and book illustrations for today's lesson.

Say **When God made the sea creatures, God saw that it was good! Let's say those Bible Words and clap our hands in rhythm. God saw that it was good!** Repeat the Bible Words activity from the previous lesson. Clap on *saw*, *it*, *good*, and then clap twice at the end.

Now let's fold our hands and thank God for all the sea creatures He makes. They are His gifts to us. Have children repeat the words of the prayer after you. Pause at the * and repeat the words with them.

Pray **Thank You, God, for fish.***
Thank You, God, for whales.*
Thank You, God, for dolphins.*
Thank You, God, for sea horses*
And for everything that lives in the water.*
Thank You for Jesus, our Savior and Friend.*
We love You, God.*
Amen.*

Liturgy Link

Listen to "Thank the Lord and Sing His Praise" (CD, track 25) on the CD. Sing along a few times as the group moves to the snack table.

Snack Time

Provide wet wipes for parents to clean the children's hands. Sing the echo prayer "Thank You, God, for This Food" (CD, track 15).

Serve cheese-flavored and/or multi-colored fish crackers and water today.

Alternative snack: Jell-O jigglers fish shapes

3 We Live
10 minutes

Growing through God's Word—Parent Talk

Children and Feelings

Lead parents through the following dialogue and questions. If you have a team leader, he or she may take the children to an area of the room to have a short playtime or to hear additional storybooks related to today's Bible lesson.

Say Think of emotions and list them on a chart or white board. **Which emotions are usually the easiest for people to express? Most difficult? How do we hide our emotions? Now think of emotions your child expresses freely. Which emotions are difficult to identify? And what might your child do to hide these emotions?**

Emotions we feel as adults are also felt by children—happiness, sadness, fear, anxiety, disappointment, loneliness, anger, surprise, and more. We might be able to identify the emotion we feel, but young children cannot. Young children need help first in identifying the emotion they are feeling, then in learning how to express that emotion appropriately. For example, simply telling a child who has grabbed another child's toy to give it back will not help her to learn to cope with the emotion or give her a strategy for dealing with it.

It's important to recognize that because we're born in and live in sin, we have negative emotions, hurtful feelings, sadness, anger, and more. God speaks to these feelings as well as positive emotions. Identify emotions and God's promises from James 1:19–20; Galatians 5:19–20; Philippians 4:6; Psalm 42:5–6; Psalm 28:7; and John 16:22. **We can thank God for the true joy and peace He gives us through Jesus, our Savior. Joy, even in our weakness, comes as God's Word and Sacraments create and sustain our belief and trust in God's promise of forgiveness and eternal life.**

You can practice recognizing and naming emotions in one another or with other children you may have—those who are able to tell you if you are right or not.

Have children repeat what you say to state their needs and wants. This method gives them practice in problem solving as they grow and develop.

Have parents role-play the following situation to determine how they can help their children. **Your child takes a toy away from a play friend (Andrew). First, name the emotion that identifies the child's actions: "You want to play with the truck that Andrew has." Next, help your child verbalize: "Can you tell me what happened?" Third, tell your child how the other person feels: "It made Andrew sad and angry that you took away the truck." Finally, help your child use words to express what he wants: "Please give the truck back to Andrew. Now tell Andrew that you would like a turn playing with the truck. Andrew, when**

you're finished playing with the truck, would you please share it with (Colin). Thank you."

Repeat the same steps—name the emotion; put emotions into words; tell how the other person feels; and use words to express your wants or needs—to role-play other situations that happen with very young children almost daily. For example, your child wants everything she sees in a department store toy section; your child cries when you leave him with a sitter; your child throws a tantrum when she doesn't want to go to bed.

We can pray for God to guide us and trust Him to help us in every situation as we help our children grow emotionally and spiritually. God is our strength and our helper.

Move from the table back to your Singing Circle area.

4 Closing
10 minutes

Songs and Prayers

17

Ask **What did we learn today? God gives us the gift of all the sea creatures He made.** Sing "Oh, Who Can Make the Fish Swim" (CD, track 17) as you point to the page of the big book *This Is the World That God Made.*

God made the fish in the deep blue sea. (Make swimming motions.)

God made you and God made me! (Point to each other; point to yourself.)

Who makes all the fish and sea creatures? That's right! God does! God cares for them and He cares for us! Let's thank God. Have families pray with you.

Pray **Dear God,***
Thank You for making the fish*
and the whales*
and the dolphins*
and all the sea creatures.*
Thank You for Jesus, our Savior and Friend.*
We love You!*
Amen.*

20

Sing "Now It's Time to Say Good-bye" (CD, track 20)

Say Good-bye

Say **When you see a fish or a seashell, you can say "Thank You, God, for loving me!"**

Take Homes

Family Page 11

Craft Page 11

Lesson 12

God Made the World—God Made Birds

Genesis 1:20–22

Key Point

We praise and thank God for the birds He makes in His world.

Connections

Bible Words
God saw that it was good. Genesis 1:10

Faith Words
God, Jesus, maker

Catechism
The Apostles' Creed: First Article
I believe in God the Father Almighty, Maker of heaven and earth.

Liturgy
Thank the Lord and sing His praise; tell everyone what He has done.

Hymn
All Creatures of Our God and King (*Lutheran Worship* 436)

Materials Needed

1 Opening

Teacher Tools
- Nametags
- Teacher CD
- Craft Page 12: God Made Birds
- Reproducible Page 5

Other Supplies
- See "To Prepare" instructions for each Activity Center

2 God Speaks

Teacher Tools
- Teacher CD
- Sprout Puppet
- God Made the Birds Poster

Other Supplies
- Poster of Jesus
- A bag for the puppet containing a sweater, an umbrella, a wrapped snack, and a key on a key ring
- Toddler Bible
- *This Is the World That God Made* (CPH)

3 We Live

Teacher Tools
- Bible

4 Closing

Teacher Tools
- Family Page 12
- *This Is the World That God Made* (CPH)
- God Made the Birds Poster

1 Opening
30 minutes

Welcome

Print today's focus "God Made Birds" on your white board for parents to see.

Encourage parents to spend time with their children at one or more of the Activity Centers, focusing on thanking God for the many birds He has made.

Say **God cares for us and He cares for the birds. We can help care for the birds in God's world.**

Activity Centers

Bird Seed

To Prepare: Small amount of birdseed in 9 × 13-inch baking pan; small cups and funnels; small plastic containers with lids.

Cover the area with a vinyl tablecloth or a large sheet. Place one or more 9 × 13-inch pans containing a small amount of birdseed on the table. Children can use small measuring cups and funnels to pour and touch the birdseed. (Supervise children closely so they don't eat the birdseed!)

Say **God made each bird so different. God gives the birds what they need to eat. They find seeds in the woods and gardens. God makes food for us to eat too. Is the birdseed smooth or rough? Is it big or little? Thank You, God, for all the birds You made.**

Parents and children can put a small amount of birdseed into a small plastic container and then put the lid on it. Shake the container and listen to the sound.

Say **God gives us ears to hear the sounds that our shakers make. We'll use our birdseed shakers when we sing in our circle soon. Thank You, God, for giving us birds in Your beautiful world!**

Art

To Prepare: Craft Page 12: God Made Birds; bird stickers; Reproducible Page 5; sturdy craft paper or art foam; colorful feathers; magnet circles or strips.

Say **God made the whole world! He made birds and gives them to us to enjoy and care for. Thank You, God, for birds!**

As children color the "God Made Birds" page, talk about birds you see in your environment, how they make nests and where they find food. Attach bird stickers.

Say **Birds are God's gifts to us. But the best gift God ever gave us was His Son, Jesus, who died and came alive again so we can go to heaven!**

Use Reproducible Page 5 to give each child a precut foam bird shape. Use a precut sturdy paper bird shape if you don't have the art foam available. Direct parents to help their children use the glue stick to attach one or two colorful feathers to the wing of the bird. Use a Sharpie marker to make a bird's eye. Then attach a magnet strip to the back of the bird.

Say **You can put your bird on your fridge or somewhere in your home to remind you that God made birds and takes care of them.**

Play Dough

To Prepare: Use old play dough for today; cookie cutters; birdseed; plastic knives.

Cover the play dough table with a vinyl covering. Place small, low plastic containers of wild birdseed for children to feel and mix into old chunks of play dough. (You'll want to discard the play dough after it's used today.)

Say **Mix the seed into the play dough with your hands. Squish and squeeze the play dough. Use the plastic knives and cookie cutters to make bird shapes. Roll the play dough to create worms for the birds to eat. When you mix the birdseed in the play dough, is the play dough smooth? Bumpy? God makes birds, and He gives them seeds to eat. Thank You, God, for taking care of us and for taking care of all the birds!**

Discovery

To Prepare: Plastic container; cut pieces of raffia; magnifying glass; small plastic Easter eggs; a twig; a length of shiny ribbon; a small piece of fabric; a ball of dryer lint; a bird song clock (battery operated).

Bring a plastic container or a small basket of cut strands of raffia to represent the grasses and twigs that a bird would weave together to make its nest. Place items such as the following into the raffia for children to feel and discover: lengths of shiny ribbon; a small piece of fabric; a small piece of aluminum foil; a twig; two or three small plastic Easter eggs. If there is a banner or pastor's stole or other object in your church that has a dove on it, bring it to show.

Say **God gives birds feathers to keep them warm. God helps birds make nests for a place to live and to take care of their eggs until they hatch. God is so good! He takes care of the birds and He takes care of us!**

Add a magnifying glass with a handle to allow children to see the items closely.

If you have a bird song battery-operated clock, bring it for children to hear many different birds' songs.

Ask **What does the cardinal song sound like? The house wren? The dove? Which bird song is the loudest? The highest pitch? The softest song? God gives each bird a very special song to sing. Thank You, God, for Your gift of birds in the world!**

What bird do you see on this banner (or on pastor's stole)? Hold the banner or stole up for the children to see. **This white dove reminds us of the Holy Spirit who makes us holy. Have you seen the dove in church?**

Pretend

To Prepare: Two tissue tubes taped together for binoculars.

Before class, cover two toilet tissue tubes with construction paper and tape them together to create pretend binoculars. Place a few paper or art foam bird shapes around your room at the children's eye level. Hang one or two from the ceiling.

Ask **Do you see a bird in our room? Look up high. Look down low. Sometimes birds fly. Sometimes birds rest in their nests or on tree branches. Sometimes birds sleep. God made birds and He said, "It is good!"**

Bring a child-size binoculars if you have one or can borrow one. Pretend to take a hike in your room and look for birds.

Say **God gave birds wings to fly high in the sky. God helps birds find safe places to sit in trees. God takes care of birds, just as He takes good care of us.**

Books and Puzzles

Provide simple shape puzzles and books related to birds and all of God's creations on a table or on a blanket in a corner of your room.

Apostles' Creed—Follow and Do by Joni Walker, CPH (56-2336)

Transition

As families put activities away, sing "Let's Clean Up" (CD, tracks 1, 2) and other favorite songs from the CD as you gather in a Singing Circle.

Singing Circle

Children can shake the birdseed shakers as everyone sings and moves to the music.

Sing

First Article Song

Morning Prayer

All Creatures of Our God and King

1 Peter 5:7

Isaiah 43:1

Good Morning to You

Happy Birthday or **God Made Me His Child** to celebrate special occasions.

Oh, Who Can Make a Flower (Variation: "Oh, Who Can Make the Birds Fly." Move your arms to each side as if you are flying.)

He's Got the Whole World in His Hands (Variation: "He's Got the Red Birds and the Blue Birds in His Hands"; add colors: yellow birds and the black birds.)

God Is So Good (Variation: "God makes the birds.")

Jesus in the Morning (Praise Him, Praise Him)

2 God Speaks
10 minutes

Come to the Worship Center

Play "All Creatures of our God and King" (CD, track 3) as parents and children gather and sit on a special rug or blanket. Sing softly with the music.

Say **I'm so glad you're here!** Welcome each child by name. **You sang so nicely! God loves to hear us praise and thank Him. He made**

such a wonderful world, and He made you and me. Aren't we glad He takes good care of us and His world? Say and do "Open Them, Close Them" as you help children settle quietly.

In the name of the Father and of the Son and of the Holy Spirit. Amen. Make the sign of the cross as you say these words and invite the parents and children to join you.

Introducing God's Word

Sprout comes carrying a bag containing a sweater, an umbrella, a wrapped snack, and a key on key ring.

Sprout: Hi, everybody!

Teacher: Good morning, Sprout! What did you bring in your bag today?

Sprout: I brought some things to help take care of you. It has been windy, chilly, and rainy lately.

Teacher: Let's see what's in your bag. *(Ask a child to take out the first item.)*

I see you've brought me a sweater! Thank you, Sprout!

Sprout: The sweater will help you keep warm in case you get cold. *(Ask a child to take out the second item.)*

Teacher: I see you've brought me a snack! Thank you!

Sprout: You can eat the snack when you get hungry. *(Ask a child to take out the third item.)*

Teacher: And you've brought me an umbrella! That's so nice of you, Sprout!

Sprout: The umbrella will keep you dry when it rains. *(Ask a child to take out the final item.)*

Teacher: And the last thing in the bag is a key to my house. Thank you, Sprout!

Sprout: You can use the key to open your door so that you can be safe and warm.

Teacher: Sprout, thank you for taking such good care of me today!

Sprout: You're welcome. But who will take care of the birds outside? Who will make sure they are warm or that they get something to eat?

Teacher: God takes good care of the birds He made, Sprout. And if God will take care of the birds, He will surely take good care of us. The birds are God's gifts to us! We can help take care of birds too.

Sprout: Daddy put birdseed in the feeder yesterday. I helped him by scooping the seeds out of the bag! Our birds in the backyard have a lot of food now! I'm going outside now to watch the birds. See you all next time. Bye now!

Teacher: Bye, Sprout!

Telling God's Word

Say Hold the Toddler Bible open as you say, **God's book, the Bible, tells us that God made all the birds and gives them to us to help care for in His world. God takes good care of the birds and God**

takes good care of us. Point to the poster of Jesus. **But the greatest gift God gives us is Jesus, who died on the cross and came alive again! Because He did that, we can go to heaven someday! How do we know all this?**

God's Word is written down. It's really true. We thank God for the Bible! Sing "Written Down" (CD, track 19) to help children grow to learn that God's Word is very special and true and we thank Him for it.

Show the God Makes the Birds Poster. Ask children to point to birds and say their names if possible. Use colors to help identify birds (*pink* flamingos, *red* cardinals, etc.). Use *big* and *small* to identify birds.

Say **God gives us sweaters and jackets to keep us warm.** Show the sweater Sprout brought for you. **How does God help the birds stay warm? He gives them feathers! God is so good!**

God gives us umbrellas to keep us dry when it rains. How does God help the birds stay dry? He helps them find tree branches and bushes where they can sit when it rains. God is so good!

God gives us a house to live in where we are safe and warm. How does God help the birds find a place to live? He helps them build nests where they can be safe. God is so good!

God gives us food to eat when we get hungry. How does God help the birds when they get hungry? He helps birds find berries, seeds, worms, and bugs to eat! Isn't God good? He takes care of the birds and He takes care of you and me!

Sing "1 Peter 5:7" (CD, track 21).

Say **When God made all the birds, God saw that it was good! Let's say the Bible Words and clap our hands in rhythm. God saw that it was good!** Repeat the Bible Words activity from the previous lesson. Clap on *saw*, *it*, *good*, and then clap twice at the end.

Now let's fold our hands and thank God for all the birds He makes. Have children repeat the words of the prayer after you.

Pray
Thank You, God, for blue birds.*
Thank You, God, for cardinals.*
Thank You, God, for flamingos.*
Thank You, God, for owls.*
Thank You, God, for all the birds You make.*
Thank You, for Jesus, my Savior and Friend.*
Amen.*

Say **We thank and praise God for making the world, for making us, and for His Word—for His Living Word, Jesus Christ.**

Liturgy Link

Play "Thank the Lord and Sing His Praise" on the CD (track 25). Encourage children to sing along.

Snack Time

Provide wet wipes for parents to clean the children's hands. Sing the echo prayer "Thank You, God, for This Food" (CD, track 15).

Have parents put a small amount of cereal-o's and raisins on each child's napkin today. Provide small cups of water or apple juice.

Alternative snack idea: Have children make a bird's nest on a paper plate by emptying a zipper bag of dry chow mein noodles as the nest "twigs." Then add a few grapes (cut in half for safety) for the bird's eggs. Add a gummy worm to remind children that God provides food for the birds He makes.

3 We Live
10 minutes

Growing through God's Word—Parent Talk

Separation Anxiety in Very Young Children

Lead parents through the following dialogue and questions.

Read Psalm 61:1–2.

Say **Baby birds left alone in their nest as their mother searches for food cry aloud in fear and anxiety. Think of a time when you were overwhelmed. Maybe you started a new job, moved, became a blended family, experienced a loved one's death or a major life change recently. How did you have your anxieties eased and what comfort did you look for?** Then read the remainder of the psalm. **Even before God made us, He knew us, loved us, and had plans for us. When we become anxious or fearful, God reminds us that we can take refuge in Him in prayer and that He will save us from sin, death, and the devil—our enemies. He brings us into His presence forever through our Baptism and through Jesus' death and resurrection.**

Read Matthew 6:25–34.

How does your child react to new places? To new people? To what or whom does he or she look for comfort?

Given a little understanding of your own reaction to changes in your life, how might you help your child in a new situation?

Separation is a major issue for young children and parents. The ultimate goal is a healthy separation, one that instills feelings of trust in children when they step from the known into an unknown. A healthy separation gives children a sense of safety rather than anxiety. This isn't an easy process for a lot of children. Even those who appear unaffected may be physically in one place and psychologically with the absent parent.

Very young children have limited experiences. How does your child express his or her fear? Being uncomfortable? How do children express their thoughts about "Will Mom or Dad come back? Who will take care of me? How will I get back home?"

What are some ways we can prepare young children for new experiences? How can we help them so they will be less anxious? Share ideas among the group. Add these:

- Tell your child what will happen, what he or she can look forward to doing, seeing, or hearing.
- Pray with and for your child, that God would be her helper and ease her anxiety.
- Visit a place ahead of time.
- Speak positively about the new situation.

- Reassure your child that you will return.
- Give your child something to keep with him—a photo of you, a key chain, or another personal item.
- Allow your child to keep a favorite blanket or stuffed animal or doll.
- Always remind her of God's constant love and care.

When you're at home, playact leaving your child at a sitter's house or a day care. Hug and say "I love you and I'll be back. Jesus loves you, and He is with you and me." Say and do these same things when the separation is real. Ask parents to share how they have handled times of separation.

Keep a ritual when you say good-bye to your child. Hug, kiss on the forehead or nose, hold hands. Tell your child, "Jesus is with you and me. I will be back. I love you too."

Keep any separation anxiety problems in your prayers. God hears and answers your needs. Give your child time, because with time, separation anxieties fade as trust grows.

Move from the table back to your Singing Circle.

4 Closing
10 minutes

Songs and Prayers

17

Ask **What did we hear from God's Word today? God made all the birds and takes good care of them.** Sing "Oh, Who Can Make the Birds Fly" (CD, track 17) as you point to the God Made the Birds Poster.

Who makes all the pretty birds in the sky and in the trees? God does! He takes care of them and He takes care of us! Let's thank God. Have families pray with you.

Pray **Dear God,***
Thank You for making all the birds*
and for taking good care of them.*
Thank You for caring for us!*
Thank You for Jesus, our Savior and Friend.*
We love You!*
Amen.*

20

Sing "Now It's Time to Say Good-bye" (CD, track 20

Say Good-bye

Say **When you use your eyes and ears to see and hear birds, you can say, "Thank You, God, for the birds You made!"**

Take Homes

Family Page 12

Craft Page 12

Lesson 13

God Made the World—God Made Animals

Genesis 1:24–25

Key Point

We praise and thank God for all the animals He makes.

Connections

Bible Words
God saw that it was good.

Faith Words
God, Jesus, maker

Catechism
Apostles' Creed: First Article
I believe in God the Father Almighty, Maker of heaven and earth.

Liturgy
Thank the Lord and sing His praise; tell everyone what He has done.

Hymn
All Creatures of Our God and King (*Lutheran Worship* 436)

Materials Needed

1 Opening

Teacher Tools
- Nametags
- Teacher CD
- Craft Page 13: God Made Animals
- Reproducible Page 6

Other Supplies
- See "To Prepare" instructions for each center
- Scarves, ribbons, birdseed shakers, rhythm instruments

2 God Speaks

Teacher Tools
- Teacher CD
- God Made the Animals Poster
- Sprout puppet

Other Supplies
- Poster of Jesus
- Sunglasses for Sprout
- Play camera
- Toddler Bible
- *This Is the World That God Made* (CPH)

3 We Live

Teacher Tools
- Bible

4 Closing

Teacher Tools
- Family Page 13
- God Made the World Poster
- *This Is the World That God Made* (CPH)

1 Opening
30 minutes

Welcome

Print today's Bible story focus "God Made Animals" for parents to see as they come into the room. Remind parents to spend time with their children at one or more of the Activity Centers, focusing on thanking God for the variety of animals He has made.

Activity Centers

Rice

To Prepare: rice; scoops; container; plastic animals.

Cover the rice pan area with a vinyl tablecloth or a large sheet. Place a few inches of rice in the container along with a few plastic scoops. Add plastic animals.

Ask **What is this animal? Can you name this one? Let's cover the animals with rice. Can you find the horse? The elephant? The dog? God made so many different animals! What animal is your favorite?**

Art

To Prepare: Craft Page 13: God Made Animals; animal stickers; cotton balls; one brown or white paper lunch bag per child; Reproducible Page 6; one large piece construction paper per child; precut animal pictures from magazines.

Talk about God's gift of animals to His world as children scribble-color the "God Made Animals" page. Add animal stickers. Glue cotton balls to the sheep and the rabbit's tail.

Say **God made all the animals in the world!**

Parents can help children glue the precut construction paper animal features from Reproducible Page 6 to the paper bag to create a simple puppet. Have everyone make the same animal, or provide a few different animal features for a variety of puppets.

Ask **Are a rabbit's ears long or short? What sound does a dog make? Look at the long whiskers on your kitty puppet! God made each animal so different. Thank You, God, for all the animals!**

Fold the construction paper in half to make a four-page booklet. Have parents and children glue a variety of animal pictures on each page. Print on the front cover "God Made Animals" and print "Thank You, God, for Animals" on the inside pages.

Play Dough

To Prepare: Play dough in a variety of colors; animal cookie cutters; small plastic animals.

Cover the area with a vinyl covering. Have parents show children how to roll play dough to flatten it. Use animal-shaped cookie cutters to make animals.

Say **God made each animal different. The giraffe has a very long neck for eating leaves off high tree branches. The cat can walk**

on a balance beam. A hippo can stay under water for a very long time. Each animal God made is so special.

Press the plastic animals' feet into the dough to make footprints.

Say **God made animals to move in many different ways. Look how big the elephant's feet are! Look how small the feet of turtles are! Some animals walk; some crawl; some run; other animals leap! How do you like to move?**

Discovery

To Prepare: "God Made the Animals" game; animal crackers for markers; small pet in its cage; pictures or real items related to animals and their care.

If possible, before class, laminate the "God Made the Animals" game page to preserve this activity for future classes. Play this game with the entire group of parents and children. Provide animal crackers to use for the markers. Give each child a "God Made the Animals" page. Children can take turns naming an animal and waiting for everyone to mark it with a cracker.

Say **God made some animals big! He made some animals small! God made the whole world!** Have parents and children tell about any animals that they have at home and how they care for them.

If a family volunteered to bring a pet hamster to class (or another small pet in a cage), have them tell what their hamster needs to live and how they take care of it.

Say **God has made your pet so special. Its soft fur keeps it warm. It gets exercise on its spinning wheel. God made hamsters to be active at night. They like to run when we like to sleep!**

Bring items (or magazine or book pictures) related to animals for children to touch and handle, such as a horse's bridle, a fur skin, antlers or horns, grooming tools, a dog's or cat's toothbrush and toothpaste, and so on.

Ask **What does this animal have on its head? God made some animals with horns and antlers. Feel (or see) how this animal's fur is so soft. God helps animals stay warm and dry. Dogs and cats need to have their teeth kept clean. God made many different animals in many different ways.**

Pretend

To Prepare: A variety of stuffed animals; empty dog and cat food boxes; clean pet water and food dishes; leashes; or any other pretend pet care items.

Children can pretend to care for the stuffed animals you have provided in an area on the floor. Provide clean water and food dishes, empty cat or dog food boxes, a leash or two.

Say **Pets need a place to sleep, don't they? Where will your pet sleep? What will your pet eat? Pets need exercise too. Will you take your pet for a walk? Pets need people to take care of them. God takes care of the animals. You are God's helper when you take care of your pets! Pets are God's gifts to us.**

Pretend to go on a hippo hunt. Tell the hippo hunt story as you walk around your room. Families should repeat your words and do each action suggested by the words.

Say **We're going on a hippo hunt. Follow me! Let's put on our hats on. Let's put on our boots. Let's put on our backpacks. Let's**

carry our binoculars. Let's carry our water bottles. We walk up a hill. We walk down a hill. We crawl through a tunnel. We run through a jungle. We wade through a stream. We're almost there! We see monkeys in the trees. We see giraffes in the grass. We see snakes on the ground. We see elephants thundering across the plain. We stop at a lake. Look, look! We see hippos drinking water! We watch them through our binoculars. Thank You, God, for the beautiful hippos! Now we go home. Say and do all the words and actions in reverse order to get you back home again. Then say: **What a fun hippo hunt we had!**

Books and Puzzles

Provide simple shape puzzles and books related to animals and all of God's creations on a table or on a blanket in a corner of your room. Here are some suggestions.

Apostles' Creed—Follow and Do by Joni Walker, CPH (56-2336)

Wooden Zoo 8-Piece Peg Sound Puzzle by Melissa and Doug (available at a teachers' store; animals make sounds when placed into the puzzle)

All God's Creatures by Karen Hill, Little Simon Inspirations, 2005

My Little People Farm Lift the Flap Book, by Doris Tomaselli, Reader's Digest Books, 1997

Who Says Moo? by Innovative Kids, 2005

Happy Baby: Kitten and Friends or *Happy Baby: Puppy and Friends*, both are *Touch, Feel and Say Books* from Priddy Books

God Gave Us You by Lisa Tawn Bergren, WaterBrook Press, 2001

Transition

Sing "Let's Clean Up" (CD, tracks 1, 2) and favorite songs from the CD as families put away activity items and move to the Singing Circle. During any transition time play "Thank the Lord and Sing His Praise" (CD, track 25) to raise families' awareness to the liturgy.

Singing Circle

Provide scarves, ribbons, or birdseed shakers for rhythm makers today.

Sing **First Article Song**

Morning Prayer

All Creatures of Our God and King

1 Peter 5:7

Isaiah 43:1

Good Morning to You

Happy Birthday or **God Made Me His Child** to celebrate special occasions.

Oh, Who Can Make a Flower (Variation: "Oh, Who Can Make the Animals.")

He's Got the Whole World in His Hands (Variation: "He's Got the Dogs and the Cats in His Hands.")

God Is So Good (Variation: "God makes the zebras; God makes the bears; God makes the monkeys . . . He's so good to me.")

Jesus in the Morning (Praise Him, Praise Him)

2 God Speaks
10 minutes

Come to the Worship Center

Play "Oh, Who Can Make a Flower" (CD track 17) as parents and children gather and sit on a special rug or blanket. Sing softly with the music.

17

Say **I'm so glad you're here!** Welcome each child by name. **I'm happy you came to hear how much Jesus loves you!** Point to the Jesus Poster. **We're happy to know that Jesus is always with us. Can you make the sign of the cross with me as we remember our Baptism:**

In the name of the Father and of the Son and of the Holy Spirit. Amen.

Introducing God's Word

Sprout comes wearing child-size sunglasses and carrying a play camera (or a small disposable camera).

Teacher: Good morning, Sprout! Why are you wearing sunglasses today? And what else did you bring?

Sprout: My auntie is taking me to the zoo to see all the animals! My sunglasses will help me see them better if the sun is bright. And I'm going to take pictures of the big bears. Mommy says we're going to see many animals at the zoo!

Teacher: Yes, you will, Sprout! Boys and girls, what are some animals that Sprout will see? *(Help the children name animals such as zebras, tigers, camels, deer, lions, penguins, monkeys, birds, giraffes, and more.)*

Sprout: Will I see every animal in the whole wide world?

Teacher: Not today, Sprout! God made so many different animals that they don't fit into one zoo!

Sprout: I'm glad God made animals!

Teacher: So am I. Have fun at the zoo, Sprout!

Sprout: See you all next time. Bye now!

Teacher: Bye, Sprout!

Telling God's Word

19

Say Hold the Toddler Bible open as you say, **God's book, the Bible, tells us that God makes all the birds. God's Word is written down. It's really true. We thank God for the Bible!** Sing "Written Down" (CD, track 19) to help children grow to learn that God's Word is very special and true and we thank Him for it.

Show the God Makes the Animals Poster and/or the page in the big book. **What animals do you see here?** Have children point to those they recognize. **Find the horses. How can horses help us? They can give us a ride on their backs. Find the squirrels. What do squirrels gather and bury in the ground? They plant nuts and seeds that grow into plants and trees.** Find other animals and tell about them. Emphasize that animals are God's gifts to us and He cares for them.

God made all the wild animals and the tame animals, the cows, sheep, goats, dogs, cats, and all the animals that move on the ground.

When God made all the animals, God saw that it was good! Let's say those Bible Words and clap our hands in rhythm. God saw that it was good! Repeat the Bible Words activity from the previous lesson. Clap on *saw*, *it*, *good*, and then clap twice at the end. Repeat the Bible Words and clap once or twice.

Now let's fold our hands and thank God for all the animals He makes. Have children repeat the words of the prayer after you. Pause at the * and repeat the words with them.

Pray **Thank You, God, for dogs.***
Thank You, God, for cats.*
Thank You, God, for horses.*
Thank You, God, for hamsters.*
Thank You, God, for all the animals You make.*
Amen.*

Say **Animals are gifts from God. The best gift God ever gave us is Jesus, our Savior and Friend.** Listen to "Thank the Lord and Sing His Praise" on the CD (track 25). Sing along a few times. **We thank and praise God for His Word—for His Living Word, Jesus.** Point to the poster at your worship center showing Jesus. **We want to tell others what God has done for us!**

Snack Time

Provide wet wipes for parents to clean the children's hands. Sing the echo prayer "Thank You, God, for This Food" (CD, track 15).

Have parents put a small number of animal crackers on the children's napkins. Serve water or apple juice. Talk about God's gift of so many animals for us as children name the animal crackers. Or have families create caterpillar snacks by placing halved-grapes in a line and adding raisins for feet.

Ask **What animals that God made do you like?**

During Snack Time you might read *Brown Bear, Brown Bear, What Do You See?* by Bill Martin, Jr. (Henry Holt and Co., 1983).

3 We Live
10 minutes

Growing through God's Word—Parent Talk

Children and Their Fears

Tell a short story about a childhood fear you had. Maybe you were afraid of dogs, storms, birds, a relative with a deep voice, or going to certain places. Then ask parents to share any fears they had as young children. Remind the group that David had fears and anxieties too. Read Psalm 55:1–8.

Ask **Do you continue to have any of your childhood fears in your adult life? Or other fears?** Allow parents to share. **Adults have fears as real as children's fears. Our fears are tied to sin, the sin in and around us that causes us to be fearful, the sin within us that causes us to be afraid rather than trust our Lord to take care of all our needs. Being full of fear is a sin. Because we're born in sin, we need the help only Jesus can give us.** Read Philippians 4:6. **What do God's Words remind us in this verse? How can His Word help us focus on His love and care for us? In the church's worship, the Divine Service, God feeds us with His Word as it is read and preached by the pastor and people, and He strengthens and feeds our faith with the Lord's Supper, granting us forgiveness for all our sins.** God wants us to come to Him in prayer. He is our loving Father. He promises to hear us. When we keep our eyes on Jesus, the Living Word, He conquers our fears! (Psalm 34:4). **When we doubt His ability to care for us we can ask God to forgive us and ask Him to take away that which causes us to be afraid. Isn't that great news? It's possible because of what Jesus has done for us!**

Does your child show fear of anything? Scary TV shows, certain people, big animals, and so on. **How does your child communicate his or her fears?** Read Romans 8:38–39 and reflect on the comfort these verses can give to us all.

Fear is a natural part of the anxieties of growing up. When might fear be helpful for a child and an adult? When it keeps us alert, protects us from harm.

Remember that most childhood fears occur because very young children have too little experience and a growing imagination. Their age prevents them from distinguishing between rational and irrational fears. For example, a two-year-old is just learning about cause and effect but has too little experience to know that a person cannot go down the drain with the bath water.

How can you help your child cope with fears? Help parents identify points such as these: Recognize the fear; take the fear seriously. Acknowledge your child's fear. Reassure, hug, and affirm with words such as "I'll hold you for a minute." "When I get scared, I remember that Jesus is with me." "I know that big dog scares you. Let's walk on the other sidewalk." Sing some of the Bible Words, songs, and hymns that you have been learning together in this class.

Discover WHY your child is afraid. Then give her the words to explain her fears. "The thunder is booming loud, isn't it? God makes the thunder, but it won't hurt you. It's part of the rain storm God sends."

Set up play situations to help your child playact fearful situations. Help him or her work out scary and fearful feelings and gain a sense of control over them. Stay with your child and rub his back for a few minutes during a thunderstorm or when they are afraid of monsters in the room.

Pray, say a reassuring Bible verse (The Lord is my helper; Jesus is always with me), sing a calming song ("God Is So Good"), and keep a picture of Jesus in your child's room. Remind your child of his or her Baptism, God's promise to keep him or her as His child, and that nothing can keep us from God and His love.

Our heavenly Father, who loved you so greatly that He sent His Son to suffer and die for you on account of your sin, cares for you in all things. Trust in Him!

Move from the table back to your Singing Circle.

4 Closing
10 minutes

Songs and Prayers

17, 21

Ask **What did we learn today? God makes all the animals for us and takes good care of them just as He takes good care of us!** Sing "Oh, Who Can Make the Animals" (CD, track 17) as you point to the page of the big book *This Is the World That God Made* or the God Made the World Poster. **Here are some of the animals that God made. Can you find an animal that God made and takes care of? Yes, God made the turtles, and He takes care of them.** Sing "1 Peter 5:7" (CD, track 21).

Say **Let's thank God for all the animals.** Have families pray with you.

Teacher Tip

Remind everyone to fold their hands and say the prayer words after you.

Pray
Dear God,*
Thank You for making dogs and cats,*
Zebras and horses,*
Cows and sheep,*
And all the animals.*
Thank You for taking good care of them.*
Thank You for Jesus, my Savior and Friend.* Amen.*

Sing "Now It's Time to Say Good-bye" (CD, track 20)

20

Say Good-bye

Say **Watch for ways to take good care of God's animals.**

Take Homes

Family Page 13

Craft Page 13

Lesson 14

God Made the World—God Made People

Genesis 1:26–28; 2:2–3; 2:7, 18–25

Key Point

We praise God for all the people He has made in the world.

Connections

Bible Words
God saw that it was good. Genesis 1:10

Faith Words
God, Jesus, maker

Catechism
Apostles' Creed: First Article
I believe in God the Father Almighty, Maker of heaven and earth.

Liturgy
Thank the Lord and sing His praise; tell everyone what He has done.

Hymn
All Creatures of Our God and King (*Lutheran Worship* 436)

Materials Needed

1 Opening

Teacher Tools
- Nametags
- Teacher CD
- Craft Page 14: God Made People
- Reproducible Page 7

Other Supplies
- See "To Prepare" instructions for each Activity Center
- Rhythm instruments, ribbons, scarves or birdseed shakers

2 God Speaks

Teacher Tools
- Teacher CD
- Sprout Puppet
- God Made Adam and Eve Poster

Other Supplies
- Play dough
- Poster of Jesus
- A very short rope (for puppet's jump rope)
- Toddler Bible

3 We Live

Teacher Tools
- Bible

4 Closing

Teacher Tools
- Family Page 14
- God Made Adam and Eve Poster

1 Opening
30 minutes

Welcome

Print "God Made People" on your white board. Point out the theme for today and explain that parents will want to reinforce the Bible truth with their children during the Activity Center time and throughout the new week.

Encourage parents to spend time with their children at one or more of the Activity Centers, focusing on thanking God for the gift of people He has made.

Activity Centers

Water

To Prepare: Container of water; washcloths; towels; plastic baby dolls.

Place a water container on a table covering. Provide a few small washcloths and towels one or two plastic baby dolls.

Say **Let's give the baby a bath. How nicely you wash the baby and dry him! Can you show me the baby's leg? Where is your leg? Can you move the baby's arm? Now move your arm. Point to the baby's nose. Now point to your nose. God made your arms and legs move. He made your nose to smell. God is so good!**

God made people as gifts to us. He makes us His children when we are baptized with water and the Word. Remind children how the pastor put water on our heads three times and said, "I baptize you in the name of the Father and of the Son and of the Holy Spirit." **God cares for us so much! He is our Maker and our heavenly Father.**

Rice

To Prepare: Rice in a pan or container; plastic scoops; plastic play people; plastic or wooden cross.

Cover the rice pan area with a vinyl tablecloth or a large sheet. Place a few inches of rice in the container along with a few plastic scoops. Add plastic people.

Ask **Who might this be? Which one is the daddy? Can you name this person? Can you find the baby? The mommy? The sister? Find the brother. Which ones are the grandma and grandpa? God made so many different people! Each person is God's gift to us.** Hide a small plastic or wooden cross in the pan and have children find it. **But the greatest gift God ever gave us is Jesus, who took all our sins away when He died on the cross! We're so happy Jesus came alive again!**

Art

To Prepare: Craft Page 14: God Made People; Reproducible Page 7; cardboard tubes or craft sticks; cross stickers.

Color and add cross stickers to the "God Made People" page.

Ask **Who is this person? Daddy? God made Daddy! Jesus died on**

the cross for Daddy! Thank You, God! Continue by saying other family members' names and comment on how God made, cares for, and forgives them because of Jesus, our Savior.

Before class, duplicate Reproducible Page 7 and cut around the paper people in large ovals. Give each family a set of paper people to represent their family members —daddy, mommy, sister, brother, baby, grandparents. Let the children scribble-color the people. Provide bright crayons for the clothing and crayon skin colors for the people. Remind parents that scribble-coloring is what two-year-olds do and that it is okay! Provide glue sticks for parents to help children attach each paper person to a cardboard tube or craft stick. Children can attach a cross sticker to each paper person too.

Say **God made you and He made your family. He made your daddy, your mommy, your sister, and your baby brother too. He sent Jesus to die on the cross and take away our sins. Jesus came alive again and lives in heaven now with God the Father, maker of heaven and earth. Thank You, God, for loving us so much!**

Extra: Before class, use fabric paint to print "Jesus loves (child's name)" along the top of the open edge of a pillowcase. (Find inexpensive pillowcases at discount store sales. Or ask a volunteer to sew pillowcases for throw size pillows. Wash and dry the cases before you begin to paint.)

Place a small amount of yellow tempera paint and a small amount of white tempera paint in aluminum pie tins. Have wet wipes close by. Have children wear paint smocks as parents help them to stamp a yellow sun and white moon and stars on the front of their pillowcases.

Say **These words say, "Jesus loves [Caleb]." Look at the pretty pillowcase you've made. God made the sun to shine all day. He makes the moon and stars to shine at night when we rest and sleep all night. God loves you very much! He is always with you, even when you take a nap and when you sleep all night. After God made the first people, He rested. He saw that everything He made was so good!** Place the pillowcases in safe places to dry.

Play Dough

To Prepare: Play dough scented with peppermint, vanilla, anise; people-shaped cookie cutters; a round plastic lid.

Cover the play dough table area with a vinyl covering. Have parents show children how to roll play dough to flatten it. You can scent play dough before class with about ½ teaspoon of peppermint or other flavorings.

Say **God made people. He gave people eyes. Your eyes can look at the play dough. God gave people noses too. You can use your nose to smell the play dough. God gave people fingers and strong muscles. What can your fingers and hands do with the play dough? God made you and said, "It is very good!" He cares for you so much! Make a cross shape. God loves you so much that He sent Jesus to die on the cross to take your sins away. But Jesus didn't stay on the cross! He came alive again! Thank You, God!**

Place a plastic lid on a ball of play dough and press down to flatten it. Use people-shaped cookie cutters.

Say **You're working hard to flatten your play dough and make people! Maybe you'll have to rest when you're finished making peo-**

ple. God worked hard when He made all the things in the world. When God was finished, He rested! He looked at everything He made and said, "It is very good!"

Discovery

To Prepare: Various sized boxes with lids; precut pictures from magazines showing a variety of ages of people; creation items from previous lessons; magnifying glass.

Provide a variety of boxes that have lids. Put precut magazine pictures of people of many different ages and cultures at this area. Have children discover the babies, toddlers, children, daddies, mommies, grandmas, and grandpas and sort and categorize them. They can move people from box to box to create families and then match the lids to the boxes as they close them.

Ask **Which people are the babies? The mommies? And so on. God made many people, didn't He? People are God's gifts to us. He gave us big people and small people. He gave us people from many countries and lands. God made all people. We are His children. God loves us all and cares for us!**

Encourage parents and children to look at items related to previous lessons, name them, look at them through the magnifying glass, touch and smell them. Provide feathers, pinecones, seashells, acorns, rocks, twigs, flowers and leaves, animal fur, a wave bottle, and any other items you've used during this quarter.

Say **God made each of these things when He made the world. God saw that everything He made was good and then God rested.**

Pretend

To Prepare: Small wooden or plastic dollhouse and toy people; baby dolls; doll beds; doll high chairs; plastic toy food; building blocks; a few pillows and blankets.

Talk about the different people God has made as children play with toy people and a dollhouse.

Say **God made mommies and daddies, grandpas and grandmas. God made babies, and He made you too! Who are the people in your family? Parents can help name their family members. Thank You, God, for our family!**

Children can pretend to care for baby dolls you have provided in an area.

Ask **Can you read to your baby? Feed her? God helps us take care of each other. How does your daddy take care of you? What does your mommy do to help you? Can you put your baby to bed? After God made everything in the world, He rested.**

Have two or more children and their parents help build a house or a church with the building blocks (if possible, use the large cardboard blocks).

Say **We're working hard together. Let's build a church! How tall and wide can we make our church? Good job, everyone! Whew, I'm tired! Let's rest now. After you play hard, or after you help mommy and daddy, you can listen to music and rest. Show us how you use a pillow and blanket to rest.**

Say and do the action rhyme together:

Say **Swim, little fish, in the water so clear.**
(Make swimming motions with arms and head.)
Fly, little bird, high up in the air.
(Make flying motions with arms.)
Creep, little caterpillar, creep, creep, creep.
(Wiggle index finger in creeping motion.)
Sleep, little children, sleep, sleep, sleep!
(Place head on your hands as on a "pillow.")

Books and Puzzles

Provide simple shape puzzles and books related to people and all of God's creations on a table or on a blanket in a corner of your room.

Board books and picture books about babies, toddlers, families

Books about Baptism

Holy Baptism—Follow and Do by Joni Walker, CPH (56-2334)

When I Get Bigger by Mercer Mayer, Golden Books, 1999

Here Are My Hands by Bill Martin, Jr. and John Archambault, Henry Holt and Co., 1989

Baby 1 2 3 by DK Children, 1998

Transition

Sing "Let's Clean Up" (CD, tracks 1, 2). After putting Activity Center items away, sing or hum "1 Peter 5:7" or "God Is So Good" (CD, tracks 21 or 11) as everyone comes to the Singing Circle.

Singing Circle

Provide scarves, ribbons, rhythm instruments or birdseed shakers for rhythm makers today.

Sing **First Article Song**

Morning Prayer

All Creatures of Our God and King

1 Peter 5:7

Isaiah 43:1

Good Morning to You

Happy Birthday or **God Made Me His Child** to celebrate special occasions.

Oh, Who Can Make a Flower (Variation: "Oh, Who Can Make the Moms and Dads" and "Oh, Who Can Make the Children.")

He's Got the Whole World in His Hands (Variation: "He's Got the Mommies and the Daddies in His Hands" and "He's Got the Children and the Babies in His Hands.")

God Is So Good (Variation: "God makes the girls; boys; babies; mommies; daddies; grandmas; grandpas; aunts; uncles; cousins; neighbors . . . He's so good to me!")

2 God Speaks
10 minutes

Come to the Worship Center

17

Play "Oh, Who Can Make a Flower" (CD, track 17) as parents and children gather and sit on a special rug or blanket. Sing softly with the music.

Say **Let's get our hands ready for "Open Them, Close Them."** Do the action verse together. Welcome each child by name. **I'm happy you came to hear how God made people and how He cares for us!** Point to the Jesus poster. **We're happy to know that Jesus died and came alive again, and that He took our sins away. Thank You, Jesus!**

Let's make the sign of the cross and say the invocation to begin our lesson.

In the name of the Father and of the Son and of the Holy Spirit. Amen

Introducing God's Word

Sprout comes holding a short jump rope.

Teacher: Hi, Sprout! What are you holding today?

Sprout: It's a jump rope. I've been jumping over it. It's great exercise! Watch me! *(Place the rope on the floor and have Sprout simply jump over it a few times.)*

Teacher: That's good jumping, Sprout! You're using the strong legs that God gave you.

Sprout: The girls and boys can use their strong legs to jump too!

Teacher: Did you know that God gave you strong arms too?

Sprout: Oh, yes! I can hold my baby brother with my arms, but only when I sit in a chair, Mommy says.

Teacher: Did you know that God gave you eyes, Sprout?

Sprout: Oh, yes! I can see the boys and girls with my eyes. Can you see me with your eyes?

Teacher: Yes, we can, Sprout! Encourage the children to nod their heads and say yes to Sprout.

Sprout: What else did God make so wonderfully?

Teacher: Did you know that God made our ears to hear many sounds?

Sprout: Oh, yes! I can hear you talking. I heard all of you singing so nicely too!

Teacher: God made us so that we can do so many things: *(have children do these with you)* blink our eyes, nod our heads, clap our hands, move our shoulders up and down, and even stamp our feet!

Sprout: God made us very, very good, didn't He?

Teacher: Yes, Sprout, God did. And He made us so that we are a gift to other people, and other people are gifts from God to us! God even helps us use our bodies to do nice things for people. We can help our parents. We can play with our baby sisters and brothers. We can share our toys and books with friends.

Sprout: Whew! All that makes me tired! Did God have to rest after He made everything in the world? That was a lot of work!

Teacher: Yes, the Bible tells us that God did rest, Sprout.

Sprout: I'm going to show my jump rope to my neighbor now. We'll play with it and then we'll rest! Bye, everyone!

Teacher: Bye, Sprout. We'll see you next time!

Telling God's Word

Say **Sprout was good at jumping, wasn't he?** Hold the Toddler Bible open as you say, **God's book, the Bible, tells us that God made the world, and all the people in the world!**

God's Word is written down. It's really true. We thank God for the Bible! Sing "Written Down" (CD, track 19) to help children grow to learn that God's Word is very special and true and we thank Him for it.

As you tell the Bible story, shape a lump of play dough into a generic person shape. **The Bible tells us that God took some dirt from the ground and made the shape of a man. He gave the man a head, a body, arms, and legs. Then God breathed into the shape and the man became alive! God named the first man Adam.**

Show a second play dough person already shaped. **Then God made a woman. He named her Eve. God loved Adam and Eve and He made them a family. He said, "It is very good!"**

When God was finished making everything in the world, He rested.

God made you, (say each child's name). God gave you a family to take care of you. Best of all, God gave you Jesus to take away all of your sins.

Show the God Made Adam and Eve Poster. God made Adam and Eve. God made you and me. **Each person is a gift from God to us. Thank You, God!**

After God made each thing and person in our world, God saw that it was good! Let's say those Bible Words and clap our hands in rhythm. God saw that it was good! Repeat the Bible Words activity from the previous lesson. Clap on *saw*, *it*, *good*, and then clap twice at the end.

Now let's fold our hands and thank God for all the people He makes. Have children repeat the words of the prayer after you. Pause at the * and repeat the words with them.

Pray **Thank You, God, for making Adam and Eve.***
Thank You, God, for making mommy and daddy.*
Thank You, God, for making me.*
Thank You, God, for Jesus, my Savior and Friend.*
We love You!*
Amen.*

Liturgy Link

Move to the snack table as you play and hum or sing "Thank the Lord and Sing His Praise" (CD, track 25).

Snack Time

Provide wet wipes for parents to clean the children's hands. Sing the echo prayer "Thank You, God, for This Food" (CD, track 15).

Have parents help squeeze cheese onto one or two round crackers to create smiley faces. Add two eyes and a smile. Or serve people-shaped cookies with juice or water to drink.

Say **God made you and me. He helps us do so many things! Eating healthy food helps our bodies grow strong. When we sleep at night and rest during the day, God helps our bodies stay healthy too. Thank You, God, for caring for us!**

3 We Live

10 minutes

Growing through God's Word—Parent Talk

The Importance of Rest

Read Genesis 2:2–3.

Say **Here we discover the importance of rest. After God created His world, He rested because His work was complete, perfect, or as the verse says, "very good" (1:31). Nothing empty or formless remained. We learn that God rested on the seventh day—He blessed that day and made it holy, not because He was tired, but so that He could set aside a rest day and enjoy His creation. This has come to be our Sabbath Day, our day of worship, a day to put aside work and to focus on thanking and praising our God for all He has done for us. He commands us to remember the Sabbath Day and keep it holy in the Third Commandment. Martin Luther tells us what this means in his explanation to the Third Commandment: "We should fear and love God so that we do not despise preaching and His Word, but hold it sacred and gladly hear and learn it." To keep the Sabbath is to rest in God's Word, to come to church, to receive the gifts of forgiveness, life, and salvation that we so desperately need!** Talk about your experiences observing the Sabbath or Sunday, a day of rest, since your childhood. Did you grow up going to worship together as a family? Maybe Sunday was a workday for you and you had a different day of the week off work. **Why is it important to keep God's commandment? To remember the Sabbath?**

There are other kinds of rest that we need as well. What kinds of rest can we identify? Our bodies need quality sleep, "down time" from work, prayer time, short power naps to rejuvenate during a work day, quiet time away from stress and hassles, quiet time to read or listen to music.

How many hours of sleep do you need to feel refreshed for a new day? What kind of rest during a workday helps you feel renewed?

Where do you go to be able to enjoy "refreshment, renewal, rejuvenation" from daily life? Read Psalm 16:9 and Psalm 91:1–2 as reminders of the "rest" God provides for us physically, emotionally, and spiritually. Isaiah writes about undisturbed places of rest for God's people in 32:18. Tell about your undisturbed places. Discuss the word *sanctuary* as it describes the Church; a place to flee from that which assails us—sin, death, and the devil. In God's house we rest in safety.

God promises rest for the weary—a reminder that He knows all our needs and well provides for us. Read Jesus' invitation in Matthew 11:28–30.

Sleep—or the lack of it—is one of the most discussed aspects of baby and toddler care. The quality and quantity of a very young child's sleep affects the well-being of everyone in the household, and it is often the difference between having cheerful, alert parents or members of the "walking dead." Spend time talking about sleep routines, habits, and problems the families may be having.

Offer these suggestions to help families with sleep and rest routines:

- Remember that every child is different. Establish a simple bedtime routine. Give your child a bath. Read one or two caring, loving storybooks. Say short prayers. Play a soothing CD. Leave a night light on if necessary. You'll want your child to fall asleep in his crib or bed on his own. Don't rely on TV as a babysitter, especially at night or at rest time. TV is a stimulator, not a pacifier!
- Allow your child to choose her PJ's, a doll or stuffed animal, or a special blanket, giving her a sense of control over the routine.
- Tuck your child into bed snugly for a feeling of security. Say, "Jesus is with you. He loves you and so do I."
- During the daytime, young children and adults need rest for both body and mind. Call it "quiet time" and allow them to have a favorite teddy bear or soothing music since a child doesn't always fall asleep. Simply resting is most important.

St. John wrote about eternal rest in the Lord in Revelation 14:13 (read the verse)**, a reminder of God's promise of the perfect and peaceful life we will have in heaven because of Jesus' death on the cross and forgiveness of all our sins. We can trust this promise God gives us. We can hold onto the hope of living with Jesus in heaven because of what He has done on the cross for us!**

Move from the table back to your Singing Circle.

4 Closing
10 minutes

Songs and Prayers

Ask **What did we learn today? God makes all people in His world and He takes good care of us!** Sing "Oh, Who Can Make the People" (CD, track 17) as you point to the God Made Adam and Eve Poster.

God made me and God made you!
(Point to yourself; point to someone else.)
God made daddies and mommies too!
(Point to a daddy, then to a mommy.)
Thank You, God, our maker!
(Hold your hands up in thanks.)

Let's thank God for making us and for taking good care of us. Have families pray with you. Remind everyone to fold their hands and say the prayer words after you.

Pray **Dear God,***
Thank You for making mommy and daddy,*
Thank You for making brothers and sisters,*
Thank You for making me!*
Thank You for Your love and care.*
Thank You for Jesus, my Savior and Friend.*
Amen.*

Sing "Now It's Time to Say Good-bye" (CD, track 20)

Say Good-bye

Say **When you go places, look at all the people God has made. God loves all people! God made you and He loves you! God sent Jesus to be your Savior and Friend! That's why He died and came alive again for you!**

Take Homes

Family Page 14

Craft Page 14

THIS IS THE World That God Made

Based on Genesis 1; 2:7, 18–23

Written by Martha Streufert Jander

Illustrated by Len Ebert

CPH
Concordia Publishing House

3558 S. Jefferson Avenue, St. Louis, MO 63118-3968
Manufactured in the United States of America

1 2 3 4 5 6 7 8 9 10 07 06 05 04 03 02 01 00 99 98

God made the world.

God said, "Let there be light."
And there was light.
God kept the light apart from the dark.
God called the light Day.
God called the dark Night.

This is the light for the world that God made.
And God saw that it was good.

And God said, "Let there be sky."
And there was sky.

And God said, "Let there be land."
And there was land.
The land kept the water apart from other water.

This is the sky above the world that God made.
This is the land in the world that God made.
This is the water in the world that God made.
And God saw that it was good.

And God said, “Let there be grass.
Let there be plants with seeds.
Let there be fruit trees with seeds.”

And there was grass.
There were plants with seeds.
There were fruit trees with seeds.

This is the grass in the world that God made.
These are the plants in the world
that God made.
And these are the fruit trees with seeds
in the world that God made.
And God saw that it was good.

And God said, “Let there be the sun.
The sun will shine during the day.”
And there was the sun.
This is the sun that shines above the world
that God made.
And God saw that it was good.

And God said,
"Let there be the moon and the stars.
The moon and stars will shine at night."
And there were the moon and the stars.

This is the moon and these are the stars
in the sky above the world that God made.
And God saw that it was good.

And God said,
"Let there be living creatures in the water."
And there were living creatures in the water.

These are the living creatures that live
in the water in the world that God made.
And God saw that it was good.

And God said,
"Let there be birds that fly above the earth."
And there were birds flying above the earth.

These are the birds that fly above the world
that God made.
And God saw that it was good.

And God said,
"Let there be cattle.
Let there be animals that creep on the ground.
Let there be all the other animals that live
on the earth."

And there were cattle.
There were animals that creep on the ground.
There were all the other animals that live
on the earth.

These are the cattle in the world that God made.
And these are the animals that creep on the ground in the world that God made.
And these are the other animals that live in the world that God made.
And God saw that it was good.

Then God said,
"Let us make people who are like us.
They will rule over all the animals
in the world."

And God made man and God made woman.
God breathed life into the man.
God also gave life to the woman.
The man's name was Adam.
The woman's name was Eve.

This is the man and this is the woman
that God made to rule over the world that
He made.

God looked at everything that He had made.
And God saw that it was very good.

And God rested.

WHAT DOES THIS MEAN?

Written by Carolyn Bergt

Illustrated by Kathy Mitter

Concordia Publishing House

3558 S. Jefferson Avenue, St. Louis, MO 63118-3968
Manufactured in the United States of America

1 2 3 4 5 6 7 8 9 10 08 07 06 05 04 03 02 01 00 99

Katie: I'm so glad you can go to church with me and my family tomorrow!

Tim: I'm kind of scared. I went to church once before, but I didn't understand anything. There's so much to know and so many big words.

Katie: Let's sit here so we can talk. I'll try to explain what happens at our church. My dad says that there are 6 main things to know and one is most important of all!

Katie: At the beginning of our worship service we have *Confession*. That's where we all stand and tell God we are sorry about the wrong things we have done. We ask Him to do two things: forgive our sins and change our hearts.

Tim: Wow! You mean grown-ups and kids together admit what they've done wrong? I'm not sure what to say. Is it okay if I just listen tomorrow?

Katie: Sure! And listen when the pastor says the *Absolution.* He reminds us that God forgives us because of Jesus, our Savior. And He sends the Holy Spirit to help us live God's way.

Tim: Whew! That's a relief!

Katie: That's why we're happy and we sing praise to God!

Tim: But I've got a question …

Tim: How can I know what is wrong? How can I know what is God's way to live?

Katie: That's another main thing we can learn—*The Ten Commandments.* That's God's Law and it tells us to love Him above everything, worship Him, obey our parents, not hurt people, and …

Tim: Where did you find out about all these things?

Katie: I learn about God's ways whenever someone reads the Bible or talks about it.

Tim: I'm sure glad God tells us so much in the Bible.

Katie: That's why we're happy and we sing praise to God!

Tim: But I've got another question …

Tim: Why would God forgive me and help me so much? I'm not important.

Katie: You are important to Him. God our Father loves us because He made us and everything on earth. He gives us what we need. And we especially need …

Tim: Help!

Katie: Right! So God gave us His Son, Jesus, who lived a perfect life in our place, who died on the cross to take the punishment for our sins, and who rose at Easter to give us new life and to give us …

Tim: Help!

Katie: Right again! We need help. So Jesus sends the Holy Spirit into our hearts to give us faith and to help us live God's way.

Tim: Where did you learn all this?

Katie: In the Bible—God's holy Word. And Sunday we'll all stand and say *The Apostles' Creed* to tell what we know and believe.

Tim: And that's why you're happy and you sing praise to God!

Katie: Now you've got the idea. But I think you've got another question, right? You are like a book called the catechism—full of questions. Thankfully, we have answers from God's Word.

Tim: Well, I've been thinking. God talks to us in the Bible. We talk to each other in the Apostles' Creed. When do I get to talk to God?

Katie: We can do that in prayer by ourselves, with our families, and even with a large group like at church. In a special prayer—*The Lord's Prayer*—we talk to God about many things. Jesus invites us to ask for all we need like food, forgiveness, and protection. And we know He has all the power and glory to help us.

Tim: I don't know why I was scared about going to church with you.

I can see now that God is so good to us!

Katie: That's why we're happy and we sing praise to God!

Tim: But I've got a question.

Katie: I'm not surprised about that!

Tim: Can I be sure that God loves me—Timothy?

Katie: God gave us a special gift called *Baptism* to show us His love in a special way. When the pastor uses the water together with the Word, God washes away our sins, and we become His children through faith. You can watch when my cousin gets baptized Sunday.

Tim: What a special day that will be! Something to remember!

Katie: That's why I'm happy and I sing praise to God!

Tim: But I've still got a question …

Tim: Is there more? I've learned about 5 important things. What is number 6?

Katie: Jesus wants us to always remember that He died on the cross to save us. So He gave us a celebration meal called *The Lord's Supper*. You'll see that on Sunday, too. The Lord's Supper has bread and wine, together with the special blessing of Christ's body and blood.

Tim: What does *this* mean?

Katie: It means that Jesus is right there with us in a special way and He blesses and forgives us! We remember all that He did to save us from sin.

Tim: So that's why we're happy and we sing praise to God!

Katie: Right! Now I've got a question …

Katie: What do you think is the one thing that's most important?

Tim: I know what it is—it's Jesus! He loves me, forgives me, and saves me.

Katie: Now you understand what being a Christian means.

Tim: And I can tell that it's not just something that happens in church.

Katie: We have Jesus with us wherever we are. With His help,
God's way is the way we live!

HOLY
BIBLE

Growing in Christ
Poster 15: Jesus
Parents & Twos
All Lessons
© 2006 Concordia Publishing House
Printed in USA R17-44-1011
Painting by Greg Copeland. © CPH.

Growing in CHRiST
Poster 14: God Made the World
Parents & Twos
All Lessons
© 2006 Concordia Publishing House
Printed in USA R14-44-1011
Painting by Robert Papp. © CPH.

Growing in CHRIST
Poster 13: God Made the Animals
Parents & Twos
Lesson 13

Printed in USA R13-44-1011

Growing in CHRIST
Poster 12: God Made the Birds
Parents & Twos
Lesson 12
© 1997, 2006 Concordia Publishing House
Printed in USA R12-44-1011

Poster 11: God Made the Sea Creatures
Parents & Twos
Lesson 11

Printed in USA R11-44-1011

Growing in Christ

Poster 10: God Made the Sun, Moon, and Stars
Parents & Twos
Lesson 10

Printed in USA R10-44-1011

Growing in Christ

Poster 9: God Made the Plants
Parents & Twos
Lesson 9

Printed in USA R09-44-1011

Poster 8: God Made the Water
Parents & Twos
Lesson 8

Printed in USA R08-44-1011

Growing in CHRIST™

Poster 7: God Makes Me His Child in Baptism
Parents & Twos
Lesson 7

Printed in USA R07-44-1011

Poster 6: God Made My Hands to Touch
Parents & Twos
Lesson 6

Printed in USA R06-44-1011

Poster 5: God Made My Mouth to Speak, Sing, and Taste
Parents & Twos
Lesson 5

Printed in USA R05-44-1011

Poster 4: God Made My Nose to Smell
Parents & Twos
Lesson 4

Printed in USA R04-44-1011

Poster 3: God Made My Ears to Hear
Parents & Twos
Lesson 3

Printed in USA R03-44-1011

Growing in Christ
Parents & Twos

Fall Teacher Kit

ISBN 13: 978-0-7586-1288-5
ISBN 10: 0-7586-1288-5

9 780758 612885

44-1011